I0761291

Artists & Authors

Books by Charles Scribner III

The Triumph of the Eucharist: Tapestries Designed by Rubens
Rubens
Bernini
The Shadow of God: A Journey Through Memory, Art, and Faith
Home by Another Route: A Journal of Art, Music, and Faith
Sacred Muse: A Preface to Christian Art & Music
Scribners: Five Generations in Publishing
Artists & Authors: A Life in Good Company

Translations

Kirsten Liese, *Elisabeth Schwarzkopf*
Kirsten Liese, *Wagnerian Heroines*
Kirsten Liese, *Maestro Muti*

Complete Bibliography: www.CharlesScribner.com

Artists & Authors

A LIFE IN GOOD COMPANY

CHARLES SCRIBNER III

Essex, Connecticut

An imprint of The Globe Pequot Publishing Group, Inc.
64 S Main St.
Essex, CT 06426
www.GlobePequot.com

All photos are from the author's collection/public domain.

British Library Cataloguing in Publication Information available

Library of Congress Cataloging-in-Publication Data

Names: Scribner, Charles, 1951– author
Title: Artists & authors : a life in good company / Charles Scribner III.
Other titles: Artists and authors
Description: Essex : Lyons Press, 2026. | Includes bibliographical references.
Identifiers: LCCN 2025030130 (print) | LCCN 2025030131 (ebook) | ISBN 9781493093632 cloth | ISBN 9781493093762 epub
Subjects: LCSH: Scribner, Charles, 1951– | Publishers and publishing—United States—Biography | BISAC: LITERARY COLLECTIONS / Essays | BIOGRAPHY & AUTOBIOGRAPHY / Editors, Journalists, Publishers | LCGFT: Essays | Autobiographies
Classification: LCC Z473.C46 A78 2026 (print) | LCC Z473.C46 (ebook)
LC record available at https://lccn.loc.gov/2025030130
LC ebook record available at https://lccn.loc.gov/2025030131

∞™ The paper used in this publication meets the minimum requirements of American National Standard for Information Sciences—Permanence of Paper for Printed Library Materials, ANSI/NISO Z39.48-1992.

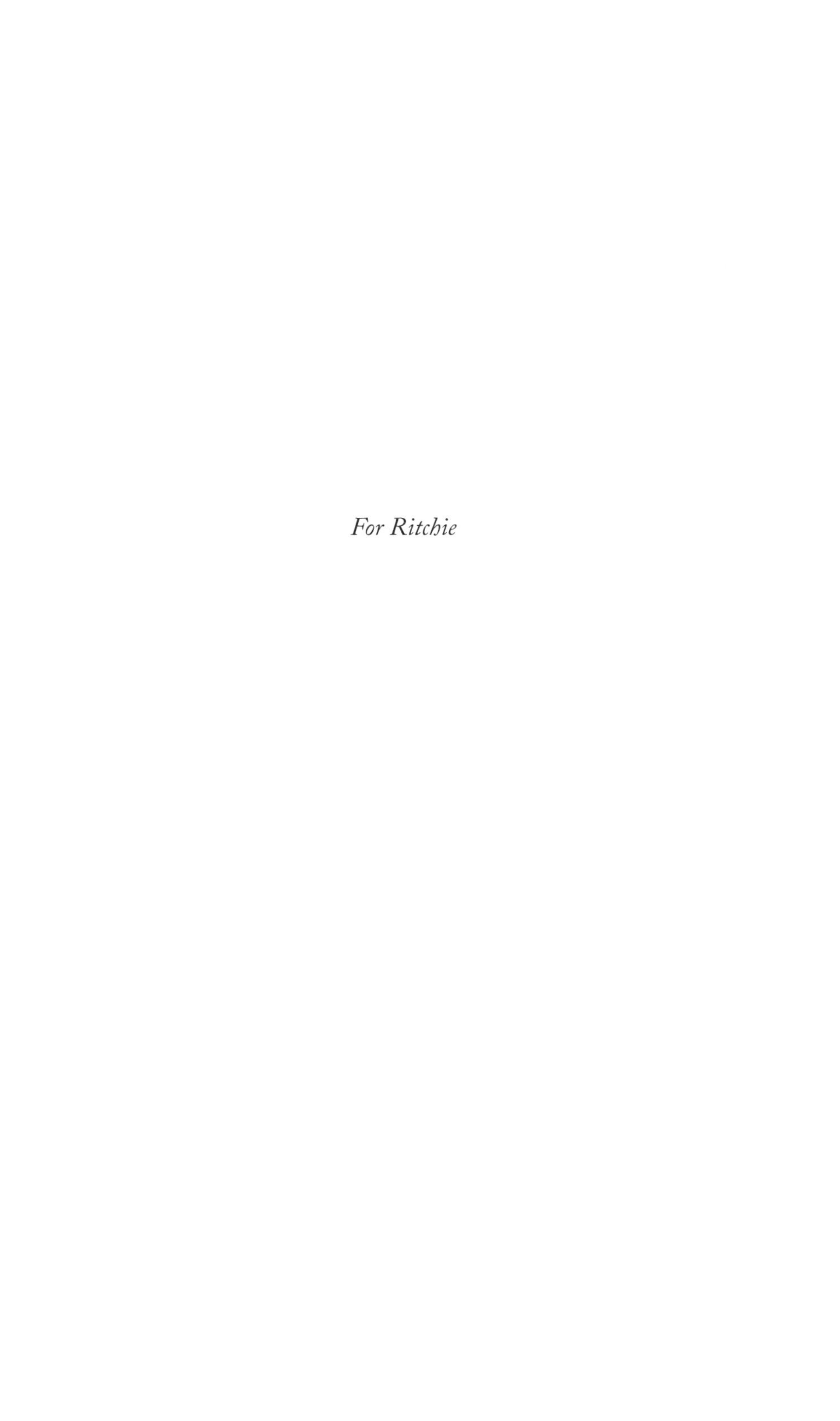

For Ritchie

Contents

Bernini, *Gloria* (1657–1666, St. Peter's, Rome)

You use a glass mirror to see your face;
you use works of art to see your soul.

—George Bernard Shaw

Preface

Lux Umbra Dei

My father, a classics major, first introduced me to the Latin maxim *Lux Umbra Dei* as an inscription to post on my senior-thesis study carrel in Princeton's art library in 1972. I don't recall him ever telling me where he got it, but after I used *The Shadow of God* as the title of my spiritual journal published in 2006, Princeton President Emeritus Robert F. Goheen wrote to me that my dad and his fellow trustees had presented him with a bronze sun dial with that Latin inscription on his retirement earlier that summer. It had a provenance close to home.

Decades later, the internet led me to Sir Thomas Browne for the English version. Then I found its source, not surprisingly, in Plato. But long before Plato, the anonymous author of the book of Genesis reflected on the special relationship between light and God. The very first command is "Let there be light." The first act of creation: "And he saw that it was good." In the New Testament, Jesus calls himself the "Light of the World." The Nicene Creed is even more explicit about that divine equation: "God from God, Light from Light." That Light is not a creation, not the light we know around us as described in Genesis. Rather, it is what Saint Paul calls "unapproachable light"—too bright for our imagination, much less our eyes. Sir Thomas Browne framed this mystery as a paradox worthy of the metaphysical poets: "Life itself is but the shadow of death . . . and light but the shadow of God."

Over the past fifty years of my art history studies, that image has had for me a deep resonance, especially for one so steeped in the art of the Baroque, which expressed as never before (or after) the *metaphysical* qualities of light—from Caravaggio's chiaroscuro to Bernini's channeling of natural light within his sculptural creations. The most radiant and dazzling of all remains Bernini's golden sunburst window in the apse of Saint Peter's in Rome, seen in the frontispiece of this book. At the far end of that long basilica, the oval window, framed on entry by Bernini's huge *Baldacchino*, transmutes actual sunlight into a spiritual and miraculous *Gloria* of gilded bronze shafts and golden stucco angels: *Gloria in excelsis Deo*.

The radiance bursts forth like a divine dawn. Yet it contains an evocative and inherent contradiction. Unlike most churches and cathedrals, this basilica at the heart of Christendom faces not east but west. So that blazing *dawn* of the sun through the stained alabaster window occurs each day toward evening, at *dusk*. This simple observation underscores the ambiguity of the frontispiece that I have given the essays herein, a collection of personal reflections over the past half century—from my graduate studies to the present. The process of revisiting and revising them has been itself an adventure in rediscovery and recapitulation. As Montaigne put it—and my father passed along to me as a student—"I have no more made my book than my book has made me."

Books & Company

Everett Raymond Kinstler, *Portrait of Charles Scribner, Jr.* (1975, author's collection, New York)

Chapter I

Digging for Diamonds

A Father's Tutelage

The summer of 1992, I spent several pleasant days sorting family and publishing files bound for the Scribner Archives at the Princeton University Library. I suppose it was this task as much as any latent nostalgia that prompted me to clean out my own storage boxes of letters and other memorabilia. In the process, I stumbled on a small treasure: a bundle of letters from my father to me at boarding school. His aim in these letters—beyond relaying family news and entertaining morsels for adolescent consumption—was to entice his son into his web of scholarly interests; at the same time, he sought to steer him away from the less benign webs in which young students are occasionally apt to get caught. His prevailing tone of bemused concern was struck at the close of his very first letter: "Keep reading on your own! Nothing will help you more scholastically in the long run. And do please remember that you read other books last summer than the 007 James Bond series."

No sooner had my father received my schedule of classes at St. Paul's—where he had preceded me three decades earlier, as his father had him (ours is a repetitive family)—than he wrote to reassure me about its implications:

> *I studied your schedule with the greatest interest, and it didn't seem too bad! Saturday morning looked pretty filled up, but perhaps you can do some of that homework before Friday night. Of course, I really don't know how much homework they give you. Every now and then I dream that I am back in school or college as a student, and despite my protests that I have graduated it never seems to make much impression. Sometimes it all seems much harder the second time around, as I am sure I would find it now. And in my dreams, I never seem to be able to get my homework done—particularly when it comes to something really major like a senior thesis at college. They say that people who have nightmares like this really did very well and were conscientious when they were students. But do not let the prospect of future bad dreams discourage you! It's all part of the price you have to pay for making an extra effort, but it's really worth it, despite the ancient Greek motto:* meden agan *(Don't overdo it).*

He had already persuaded me to sign up for ancient Greek, in addition to Latin, in my first year at the school. His deep love of the classic languages is one of the golden threads of his web of ideas. My first Greek assignment—learning the new alphabet—was tearful. But I soon recovered. He rushed to bolster my decision to stick with it: "I am glad that you do not find Greek quite as impossible as it seemed at first appearance. It is the most beautiful language, and the things you will read in Greek were the models for the literature of later periods. You will never be sorry you took Greek, I promise you."

By the end of the school year, I was fully sold on Greek. But in picking courses for the next year, I had planned to drop Latin—without his prior consultation—and this decision almost created an international crisis: "As for dropping Latin next year," he wrote,

> *I really think it would be a mistake to have gone this far with Latin only to drop it now, and if I ever expected you to do that, I never should have advised you to start Greek. Please let me know if it was your understanding to drop Latin only temporarily, that is, for the next year. If that is your plan, I'll be glad to stay out of the discussion. Otherwise, I really should like to find out more about the program you are mapping out. Needless to say, I am very keen about Greek, and again feel it would be a great mistake not to carry on with that too. Also, you should have a taste of a good science course before you get to college. But it would be very unwise for you to drop Latin for good at this point. Please write your father a reassuring letter about this or call him as he is most disconcerted!*

Two weeks passed, after which he wrote:

> *Not having heard any more about the schedule of courses, I telephoned Mr. Hall to register my doubts as to the wisdom of dropping Latin for good at this point. . . . I really would never have ventured to get you to take up Greek if I had thought it would be at the price of dropping Latin . . . although possibly you could get away with skipping a year of Latin. I don't know about that. In any case I judge that you really do appreciate the fascination and beauty of the Greek language. The literature is probably the greatest treasure of our civilization, and I know that you will always be grateful for getting to know it in its own tongue.*

His prediction was on the mark: I was to continue reading Greek for the remaining three years of school and the first two years of Princeton before being seduced for good by art history.

My father's letters likewise reveal his love of classical music, which he pursued via the phonograph—"his chosen instrument,"

I called it. He constantly wrote of new records he had purchased and was most supportive of my piano studies, which I had earlier intended to lead to a professional career. "I think you are wise not to bite off more than you can chew. After your studies, music is virtually an obligation in the light of the years you put into it and your own ability. You'll never really have an opportunity to master the piano later if you don't do so now. And once you have mastered it, you'll be able to keep up a repertory all your life—adding new pieces from time to time." Once again, on the mark. Though my career was never to be at the keyboard, I still find myself there after hours.

My father's literary horizons extended well beyond Scribners' roster of authors. The summer before, he had assigned me a $50 reading list of English and American classics. I got paid on completion—a hefty sum for a jobless teenager in 1965! Once at school, I got a new list—the best books I've ever read—with an occasional comment from the paternal professor: "I am delighted you liked the Chekhov stories. I was at St. Paul's when I read these first, and I still remember the impression they made on me. I thought they were beautifully written. There are so many other wonderful collections of short stories for you to become familiar with—e.g., Tolstoy, de Maupassant, Joyce, Hemingway—that I can't wait to have you start on the next fifty or seventy-five dollar list! I am also anxious to read your own story." (It was, predictably, ersatz Chekhov, about a desperately lonely boy at a Saint Petersburg prep school. Published in the *Horae Scholasticae*, it worried Mr. Greaves, my housemaster, until I reassured him that the story reflected only my reading, not my life.)

By my second year, I had immersed myself in dramatics. My first major role, Cassius in Shakespeare's *Julius Caesar*, evoked a fatherly insight: "I reread *Julius Caesar* and was surprised to find Cassius a far more sympathetic character than I remembered him. I imagine the 'lean and hungry look' has struck and prejudiced readers. The introduction to your Pelican edition of the play was especially interesting in this respect since it showed how frustrated Cassius must have been to have every practical suggestion brushed aside by the starry-eyed Brutus! Did you find that difficult to convey?" In fact, I was mildly disturbed by how easily I identified with the cynical Cassius: I couldn't fault him.

In any case, my father proceeded to prescribe a program of study for a series of prize scholarship exams I was scheduled to take, with special emphasis on how to survive Caesar's *Gallic Wars*. I'll spare you the details (three single-spaced pages) worthy of the Roman general himself. But my dad's campaign to capture the Shakespeare prize is worth quoting in full:

> *I know all of this may be time consuming, but it could help you very much, and there's nothing more nightmarish or frightening than to step into an exam unprepared. That was my own experience since I did absolutely no preparatory work at all and still remember the miserable experience of trying to answer questions on things I had completely forgotten. As a matter of fact, I was too dumb to find out what we would be examined on, and in those days no one took the initiative in briefing you beforehand. The boy who won did find out in advance and cleaned up!*
>
> *When it came to the Whipple Medal in Shakespeare, I got tricky myself and adopted the following strategy which only took a day or so: 1) reading something about the play and Shakespeare's sources and models; 2) reading the play itself three times to get the plot and structure and characters clearly in mind; 3) memorizing about a dozen passages from various parts of the play—some as short as one line, some five or ten lines. By sprinkling these throughout my answers I was able to convey the impression that I knew the entire play by heart! How could I lose—especially since I compared the alteration of sad and happy sections of the play with the third movement of Beethoven's Seventh Symphony! Naturally this particular*

plan may not be possible with the exams you will be taking, but what I want to emphasize is the effectiveness of having a "strategy," so to speak. It gives you a marvelous feeling of confidence, too, which is half the battle.

I didn't win, but there is no question that I had the best coach available. One of my stumbling blocks was solid geometry. Math and science were two of my father's primary passions—indeed, professional avocations. He wasted no time trying to get me over the hurdle: "I wish I could help you on the geometry originals. As you point out, a lot of this is confidence, and it is possible to defeat yourself if you become too anxious. Often there is some simple trick or clue to a solution. Sometimes it is seeing a familiar theorem in an unusual setting." After much about angles, arcs, diagrams, and hypotenuses, he dropped this pearl of wisdom:

In other words, do something; even if what you start to do may not be exactly right, it may put you on the track of a solution. Be sure that all the data you have in the hypothesis are brought into play. If everything in the hypothesis isn't capitalized on, it means you aren't focusing on the particular situation involved. They will almost never give you irrelevant data in the hypothesis. It might help you to work over a number of fairly difficult originals as a way of reviewing. Practice on them will build up your confidence and, like the London Times *crossword puzzles, show you some of the tricky things that may arise! Hope I haven't confused you by all these suggestions. Usually the solution to an original is very simple and straightforward once you see the essential elements of the problem.*

He must have quietly despaired when I told him that I really didn't believe for a moment Galileo's law of gravity—any fool knows that big heavy things fall faster than small light ones, right?—but for the sake of passing the physical science course, I would pretend to accept that law. Besides, I was preoccupied with my upcoming performance as Shakespeare's cavalier King Richard II. Once more unto the breach, my father charged with pen in hand:

> *Sorry you have so much trouble in accepting 16th-century science. Of course, when one deals with objects falling in an atmosphere, they are all subject to resistance or forces of air friction, and obviously a bullet falls faster than a feather. But the laws of uniform acceleration abstract from atmospheric conditions and assume a perfect vacuum. In a vacuum is there any reason to think that a cannonball (for example), which can be thought of as a kind of gluing together of tiny pellets, should fall faster than any one pellet composing it? In an atmosphere the forces act on the surface of a falling object, and since the volume and therefore mass of an object varies with the cube of a linear dimension while its surface area varies with the square, the smaller an object is made, the more it is responsive to air resistance. That's why dust floats! But your natural insincerity obviously enables you to take positions contrary to what you believe to be the case. A wonderful attribute for an actor and apparently useful in the study of physical science.*

He later reinforced his concern with a book, *The Double Helix*, on the exciting adventure culminating in the discovery of the DNA molecule. "It will only take an hour or so. I want you to have a picture of the beautiful and imaginative side of science as well as the lively, amusing personalities of some of the great creative scientists. It is also filled with English lore!" (He knew that would hook me.) His own "science gene" evidently skipped a generation. I was never at home in the lab. Once I hooked up my Bunsen burner hose to the water faucet and then panicked at the gush of "liquid gas" that shot up to the ceiling and threatened to extinguish us all—or so I feared. "Ey-uh, Scribner, did you try to light it?" chuckled the chemistry teacher, Mr. Gillespie.

As a Princeton freshman, I tried once again and took a course aptly nicknamed "Physics for Poets." Someone once said that taking physics at Princeton was like trying to take a drink from a fire hose. I was nonetheless inspired by the history of science as the history of progressively beautiful—that is, clearer, simpler, more economic—explanations of the confusing, cluttered natural world around us. My appreciation of science as a fine art finally dawned. A few years later, it proved invaluable in solving a problem in art history involving the original configuration of a Rubens tapestry cycle, *The Triumph of the Eucharist*—the subject of my senior thesis, dissertation, and first book.

My father happened to pop by my room during senior year as I was going mad rearranging Xeroxes of the tapestries (all framed by two distinct orders of illusionistic columns) on the floor, trying to decide which of the five proposed linear sequences around the Madrid convent cloister was the most likely. Then I tried something new—the architecturally obvious: arranging them in two tiers, with the elaborate Solomonic columns over the plain Doric. Eureka! It worked. Dad loved to note that "the obvious is these days often overlooked."

When asked by students, "What was the most important art course you took?" I reply, "Physics." It was worth the struggle. As Einstein said, "If you can't explain something simply, you don't understand it well enough." My father's love of science was based in art—the art of economy, simplicity. No scientific theory can claim absolute truth; the best ones are those that explain the most with the least.

I trust that, by now, the next question—"Who was your most influential teacher?"—has already been answered. Not every teacher is himself, or herself, a parent, but every parent is first a teacher. I've had the best.

While I was still a schoolboy, my father told me a parable or short tale that resonated for thirty years until, shortly before his death, I asked him where he had heard it. It had been in the St. Paul's School chapel, he replied, in a sermon by the legendary rector Dr. Drury—the only one of the weekly sermons that he remembered.

Once upon a time a young prince was making a journey alone on horseback to another kingdom. He had come a long way, and he had a long way to go. One night, as he was crossing a stream, he heard a commanding voice call to him out of the darkness: "Stop and fill up your saddle bags with the sand of this stream."

The young prince reined in his horse for an instant and deliberated. He was awed by the voice, and he wanted to obey, but he was also impatient to ride on. So, he reached down, snatched up a handful of sand from the bottom of the stream, put it in his pocket, and galloped off on his way.

The next morning, he remembered the stream and the voice and the sand. Out of curiosity he reached into his pocket, and, lo and behold, it was filled with diamonds. And so, as the story goes, the young prince was both glad and sorry. He was glad that he had stopped and taken some sand, and he was sorry that he had been impatient and not taken more.

It is the common experience—and joy—of both teachers and students alike to discover, often years later, that what first appeared as sand sparkles as diamonds.

Chapter 2

F. Scott Fitzgerald

From Princeton to Paradise

> *Reading is a means of thinking with another person's mind; it forces you to stretch your own. . . . For learning purposes there is no substitute for one human mind meeting another on the page of a well-written book.*
>
> —Charles Scribner Jr.

And that is where we meet Scott Fitzgerald, whose life and career bounced between successes and setbacks like the alternating current of major and minor keys in a Mozart symphony. He was born in 1896. Just as his life bridged two centuries, so his work has a Janus-like aspect, looking back to the Romantic lyricism and epic dreams of nineteenth-century America and forward to the syncopated jazz of the twentieth century. "My whole theory of writing," he said, "I can sum up in one sentence. An author ought to write for the youth of his own generation, the critics of the next, and the schoolmasters of ever afterward." How magnificently—if posthumously—he fulfilled that ideal. His fleeting literary fortunes—a dozen years of commercial and literary success followed by distractions and disappointments—ended in 1940 with a fatal heart attack when he was forty-four. He was then hard at work on *The Last Tycoon*, the Hollywood novel he hoped would restore his reputation. At the time of his death, his books were not (as is so often claimed) out of print with Scribners, his publisher. The truth is even sadder. They were all in stock at our warehouse and listed in our catalog, but no one was buying them.

When Fitzgerald's daughter, Scottie, first approached the Princeton University Library and offered to donate her father's papers, she was turned down. It couldn't be the repository, the librarian said, for every failed alumnus author's papers. Fortunately, she gave them a chance to reconsider several years later. Today, those archives are the most avidly consulted holdings of the library by scholars who come there, as if on pilgrimage, from all over the world. More copies of Fitzgerald's books are now sold each fortnight than during his entire lifetime. His novels and stories are studied in high schools and colleges across the country—indeed, around the world. I am the fourth Charles Scribner to be involved in publishing his works ever since my great-grandfather signed him up at the prodding of that young editor of genius Max Perkins in 1919. But three generations and namesakes later (ours is a redundant family), I am struck by the realization that I am the first generation—of no doubt as many to come—to have been introduced to this author's work in a classroom.

My grandfather, Fitzgerald's contemporary and friend as well as publisher, died on the eve of the critical reappraisal and ensuing revival of his works that gained momentum in the 1950s and has continued in full force down to the present time. It was my father who presided over that literary apotheosis unprecedented in American letters. As a fledgling editor, I had the good fortune to work closely with Fitzgerald's delightful daughter, Scottie, together with her advisor, Professor Matthew J. Bruccoli, whose prolific scholarship and infectious enthusiasm fanned the flames of Fitzgerald studies. The day I met Matt, I asked what had prompted him to devote the lion's share of his scholarly life to Fitzgerald. He told me that one Sunday afternoon during his teenage years, he was driving with his family when he heard a dramatization of *The Diamond as Big as the Ritz* on the car radio. He later went to a local library to find the story. The librarian had never heard of Scott Fitzgerald. But he finally managed to locate a copy, "and I never stopped reading Fitzgerald." This story struck a familiar chord, for I, too, remember where I was when I first encountered that same literary jewel "as big as the Ritz."

It was an evening train ride from Princeton to Philadelphia. A commute was converted into a fantastic voyage. Fitzgerald later converted my professional life, claiming more of me than any living author. There are worse fates in publishing than to be a "curator of literary classics," especially if one's own scholarly bent is in Baroque art. Placed alongside my other specialties, Rubens and Bernini, Fitzgerald seems very young indeed: a newcomer in the pantheon of creative genius.

There is something magical about Fitzgerald. Much has been written and dramatized about the Jazz Age personas of Scott and Zelda. But the real magic lies embedded in the prose and reveals itself in his amazing versatility. Each novel or story partakes of its creator's poetic imagination, his dramatic vision, his painstaking (if virtuoso and seemingly effortless) craftsmanship. Each bears Fitzgerald's hallmark: the indelible stamp of grace. He is my literary candidate to stand beside the demigods Bernini, Rubens, and Mozart as artists of divine transfigurations. The key to Fitzgerald's enchantment lies in the power of his romantic imagination to transfigure his characters and settings as well as the very shape and sound of his prose. There is a sacramental quality—one that did not wane along with formal observance of his Roman Catholic faith. I say "sacramental" because Fitzgerald's words transform their external geography as thoroughly as the realm within. The ultimate effect, once the initial reverberations of imagery and language have subsided, transcends the bounds of fiction. I can testify from firsthand experience.

When I arrived at Princeton as a freshman in the fall of 1969, I was following in the footsteps of four generations of namesakes before me. Yet, surprisingly, I did not feel at home. It seemed a big, impersonal place—more than ten times as big as my old boarding school, St. Paul's. There, I had first been exposed to Fitzgerald in English class, where we studied *The Great Gatsby*. But my first encounter at Princeton was dramatically extracurricular. One day that fall, soon after the Vietnam Moratorium and the ensuing campus turmoil, I returned to my dormitory room to find that some anonymous wit had taped to my door those infamous opening words from Fitzgerald's "The Rich Boy": "Let me tell you about the very rich. They are different from you and me." (My next-door neighbors in the dorm represented a cross section of campus radicals, and while I was hardly "very rich" by Fitzgerald's lights—closer to Nick Carraway than to Tom Buchanan—I was, as the son of a university trustee, politically incorrect.)

Stung though I was by this welcome note, curiosity got the better of me. Off I went to Firestone Library, looked up the story, and read it. Now hooked on Fitzgerald, I bought a copy of *This Side of Paradise*, his youthful ode to Princeton. Though university officials to this day bemoan its satirical depiction of their college as a country club, they miss the point: the poetry, the sacramental effect of this witty, romantic novel on their majestic campus. For me, the book infused the greenery and gothic spires with a spirit, with a soul, with life.

Fitzgerald transfigured Princeton. I now saw it not as a stranger but through the wondering eyes of freshman Amory Blaine: "Princeton of the daytime filtered slowly into his consciousness—West and Reunion, redolent of the sixties, Seventy-nine Hall, brick-red and arrogant, Upper and Lower Pyne, aristocratic Elizabethan ladies not quite content to live among shopkeepers, and topping all, climbing with clear blue aspiration, the great dreaming spires of Holder and Cleveland towers. From the first he loved Princeton—its lazy beauty, its half-grasped significance, the wild moonlight revel of the rushes." For me, it was not love at first sight, but thanks to Fitzgerald, it was love at first reading. Oscar Wilde was right: Life imitates art, not the other way around. We view our world through a prism of words. During my sojourn there, friends and I would recite in unison Fitzgerald's sonnet of farewell to Princeton: "The last light fades and drifts across the land—the low, long land, the sunny land of spires."

From his earliest days, Fitzgerald wanted nothing more than to be a writer: "The first help I ever had in writing was from my father, who read an utterly imitative Sherlock Holmes story of mine and pretended to like it." It was his first appearance in print at age thirteen. Here's the chilling dénouement, which proves that writers are made, not born:

> *"I forgot Mrs. Raymond," screamed Syrel, "where is she?" "She is out of your power forever," said the young man. Syrel brushed past him and, with Smidy and I following, burst open the door of the room at the head of the stairs. We rushed in. On the floor lay a woman, and as soon as I touched her heart I knew she was beyond the doctor's skill. "She has taken poison," I said. Syrel looked around; the young man had gone. And we stood there aghast in the presence of death.*

No surprise that he next took to writing plays, one a summer, for a local dramatics group. At Princeton, he wrote musical comedies for the Triangle Club before he flunked out (chemistry was the culprit), joined the army, and wrote his first novel, *This Side of Paradise*.

"Start out with an individual and you find that you have created a type—start out with a type and you find that you have created nothing." Fitzgerald started out with himself—a good choice. "A writer wastes nothing," he said, and he proved it by mining his early years at St. Paul and Princeton to forge his early stories, poems, and dramatic skits into the autobiographical novel that launched his fame. Fitzgerald's novel was turned down—can you believe?—twice by my great-grandfather, until, after several revisions by a young writer who refused to give up, it was published to great acclaim.

Years later, writing to his daughter, Fitzgerald offered the following advice: "Don't be a bit discouraged about your story not being tops. . . . Nobody became a writer just by wanting to be one. If you have anything to say, anything you feel nobody has ever said before, you have got to feel it so desperately that you will find some way to say it that nobody has ever found before." A couple of years later, he added some more technical advice: "All fine prose is based on the verbs carrying the sentences. They make sentences move."

Unlike Fitzgerald's brisk prose, I did not move; I stayed on at Princeton for two more degrees, leaving the university only when there were no more to be had, but not before I had the pleasure of teaching undergraduates. Since my field was art history, the next transition—into the family publishing business—was abrupt, but once again facilitated by Fitzgerald. Ensconced at Max Perkins's old desk at Scribners, I dreamed up as my first book project in 1975 a revival of Fitzgerald's obscure and star-crossed play *The Vegetable; or From President to Postman*, which featured a presidential impeachment. Ironically, the play had opened and closed in 1922 at *Nixon's* Apollo Theater in Atlantic City. My post-Watergate project not only justified repeated revisits to the Princeton University Library for research but also, and more important, brought me into a happy working relationship with Scottie. It was published during the election year of 1976, and Fitzgerald's version of a presidential address in act two—a delicious confection of mixed metaphors—still resonates to this day.

After approving my introduction to the play, Scottie wrote me a touching note about her parents' reburial service in the Catholic cemetery of Rockville, Maryland. I had been unable to attend and instead had arranged for a memorial Mass to be said that day in the once exclusively Protestant Princeton chapel. Fitzgerald would have smiled at the delicious irony of both liturgies.

"Surely it was the Princeton prayers," Scottie later wrote to me, "that made our little ceremony go so smoothly. The day was perfect; a mild breeze rustling the fallen leaves, and there were just the right number of people, about 25 friends and relatives, 25 press, 25 county and church 'officials,' and 25 admirers who just popped up from nowhere. As most of the guests had never before had Bloody Marys in a church basement, the party afterward was a jolly affair, too. I'm sorry you weren't there but loved knowing we were having a backup ceremony in his real spiritual home."

I cannot resist contrasting Scottie's gracious note with what Edmund Wilson wrote to me when I first proposed that he reintroduce the play Fitzgerald had dedicated to him. Wilson had given its publication a rave newspaper review—a fact he now chose to forget: "I cannot write an introduction to *The Vegetable*. The version I read and praised was something entirely different from the version he afterwards published, and I did not approve of this version. The trouble was he took too much advice and ruined the whole thing. I was not, by the way, as you say, closer to Fitzgerald than anybody else. I was not even in his class at college, though people still think and write as if I had been." When I lamented this letter to my father, he said that for Wilson it wasn't so bad and that "after God created the rattlesnake, he created Edmund Wilson."

Fitzgerald considered his year and a half spent on *The Vegetable* a complete waste, but I disagree, for he followed it with a new novel written with all the economy and tight structure of a successful play: *The Great Gatsby*. Both *The Vegetable* and *The Great Gatsby* shared the theme of the American Dream (first as a spoof for a comedy and finally as the leitmotif of a lyric novel). I don't think there has ever been a more elusive, mysterious, intriguing character than Gatsby. He's pure fiction and pure Fitzgerald: the hopeful, romantic outsider looking in.

> *He smiled understandingly—much more than understandingly. It was one of those rare smiles with a quality of eternal reassurance in it that you may come across four or five times in life. It faced—or seemed to face—the whole external world for an instant and then concentrated on you with an irresistible prejudice in your favor. It understood you just so far as you wanted to be understood, believed in you as you would like to believe in yourself, and assured you that it had precisely the impression of you that, at your best, you hoped to convey.*

Who cares how James Gatz became Jay Gatsby—bootlegger, or worse? Who would not want to be in such a presence?

In his first letter to Perkins—summer of 1922—about his "new" novel, Fitzgerald wrote that it would "concern less superlative beauties than I run to usually" and "would center on a smaller period of time." He was to change the period and locale as he began writing (it was originally set in the Midwest and New York around 1885), but he never abandoned his determination to limit the time frame and thus give a sharper focus to his plot and characters than he had done in his earlier two novels. And this, I think, was the result of his failed attempt to be a Broadway playwright. The special demands imposed by a play—a short work defined by acts and scenes, limited in time and setting—proved an ideal exercise in literary craftsmanship, which the young novelist sharpened through the long series of revisions while the play was in rehearsal.

From Fitzgerald's long-lost first draft of 1923, only a fragment survives in the form of the short story "Absolution" and two handwritten pages I discovered in a rare bookshop in New York. They reveal that Fitzgerald had already settled on the essential plot and locale of the final version, but the story was told in the third person. The next year, he wrote to Perkins that he was now working on a "new angle"—I'm sure he meant through the eyes of his inspired narrator Nick Carraway (it's worth streaming the famous Redford film just to hear Sam Waterston tell the story).

In the flush of creativity, Fitzgerald wrote to his editor, "I feel I have enormous power in me now, more than I've ever had in a way, but it works so fitfully and with so many bogeys because I've talked so much and not lived enough within myself to develop the necessary self-reliance. Also I don't know anyone who has used up so much personal experience as I have at twenty-seven."

Perkins, for his part, had grave reservations about the proposed title *Among the Ash Heaps and Millionaires* and suggested that Fitzgerald return to *The Great Gatsby*, which he called "effective and suggestive." He also commissioned at this early date—seven months before the author completed his manuscript—the most famous jacket painting of the past century, which we'll consider presently. Fitzgerald continued to revise his draft from September to October, "working at high pressure to finish," he wrote in his ledger. In November 1924, he mailed the manuscript to Perkins with a new title, *Trimalchio in West Egg*. He was to run through several others—*Trimalchio*, *Gold-Hatted Gatsby*, *Gatsby*, *The High-Bouncing Lover*, and *On the Road to West Egg*—before Perkins's steady favorite was restored in time for publication.

Most of the final revising was done directly on the printed galley proofs, which Fitzgerald treated almost as a clean typescript. (In fact, the uncorrected galleys, titled *Trimalchio*, were published several years ago as if a distinct novel.) Then, just three weeks before publication (April 10, 1925), the nervous author cabled his editor from Paris, "Crazy about title *Under the Red, White, and Blue*." Fortunately, it was too late to change the title, and our book was spared the fate of sounding like a George M. Cohan song.

While writing an introduction to a new 1979 paperback edition of *The Great Gatsby*, I decided to revive the original jacket—it is now an icon of the Jazz Age—and twenty years later, it was enlarged at my suggestion into a huge poster for John Harbison's opera at the Met. When Matthew Bruccoli discovered the artist Francis Cugat's preliminary sketches for his *Gatsby* dust jacket in a country shop, serendipity allowed me at last to merge art history

Original painting by Francis Cugat for *The Great Gatsby* (1924, Princeton University Library)

and literature. I'm a Gemini. This once, thanks to Fitzgerald, my dual careers came into sync.

Francis Cugat is not a household name. Born in Cuba in 1893, he was a set designer for Douglas Fairbanks in Hollywood and, decades later, a consultant to Technicolor on films including *The Quiet Man* and *The Caine Mutiny*. (He is better known as the brother of bandleader Xavier Cugat.) He designed only one jacket for Scribners and did not continue in that line of work. Yet his painting is the most celebrated and widely disseminated jacket art in twentieth-century American literature and perhaps of all time. After decades of oblivion—and several million copies later—this Art Deco tour de force has established itself as a classic of graphic art. At the same time, it represents a unique form of "collaboration" between the author and the jacket artist. Under normal circumstances, the artist illustrates a scene or motif conceived by the author; he lifts, as it were, his image from a page of the book. In this instance, however, the artist's image preceded the finished manuscript, and Fitzgerald actually claimed he had "written it into" his book.

Cugat's small masterpiece is not illustrative but symbolic and iconic: the sad, hypnotic, heavily outlined eyes of a woman beam like headlights through a cobalt night sky. Below, on earth, brightly colored lights blaze before a metropolitan skyline. Cugat's carnival imagery is especially intriguing in view of Fitzgerald's pervasive use of light motifs throughout his novel, specifically in metaphors for the latter-day Trimalchio, whose parties were illuminated by "enough colored lights to make a Christmas tree of Gatsby's enormous garden." Nick sees "the whole corner of the peninsula . . . blazing with light" from Gatsby's house "lit from tower to cellar." When he tells Gatsby that his place "looks like the World's Fair," Gatsby proposes that they "go to Coney Island." Fitzgerald had already introduced this symbolism in his story "Absolution," originally intended as a prologue to the novel. At the end of the story, a priest encourages the boy, who eventually develops into Jay Gatsby, to go see an amusement park—"a thing like a fair only much more glittering" with "a big wheel made of lights turning in the air." But "don't get too close," he cautions, "because if you do, you'll only feel the heat and the sweat and the life." Daisy's face, says Nick, was "sad and lovely with bright things in it, bright eyes and a bright passionate mouth."

In Cugat's final painting, the celestial eyes enclose reclining nudes, and the streaming tear is green like the light "that burns all night" at the end of Daisy's dock, reflected in the water of the sound that separates her from Gatsby. What Fitzgerald drew directly from Cugat's art and "wrote into" the novel must remain an open question, though I believe the best candidate is not the famous billboard eyes of Doctor T. J. Eckleburg, but rather Nick's image of Daisy, at the end of chapter 4, as "the girl whose disembodied face floated along the dark cornices and blinding signs" of New York at night. (My interpretation, as an art historian, of the documents and artwork was published by the Princeton University Library under the title "Celestial Eyes: From Metamorphosis to Masterpiece.")

The reflected lights of Gatsby—whether votive or festive—still transfigure Gatsby's island, where my family and I were transplanted after several generations on the mainland. From our new vantage point, I cannot look out over the sound without smiling at Fitzgerald's description: "the most domesticated body of salt water in the western hemisphere, the great wet barnyard of Long Island Sound." There is no longer a dock at the beach in Lattingtown, and as the crow flies we are, in fact, several miles east of East Egg. But occasionally I catch a glimpse of a green light reflected in the water, and each time I drive through the Valley of Ashes (now the site of the Citi Field stadium) and approach the twinkling Manhattan skyline, I feel very much at home. The novel has made me a native.

One wise college professor told us that the ultimate function of art is to reconcile us to life. Fitzgerald's prose is life enhancing; its evocative power endures. That is why I have no doubt he should be beaming from the other side of paradise.

Chapter 3

Tender Is the Night

Fitzgerald's Credo

To this day, F. Scott Fitzgerald's name conjures up the magic of the Jazz Age, and his immortality rests secure on his literary masterpiece, *The Great Gatsby*, which, with almost miraculous economy and flawless craftsmanship, captures in so short a volume both an era of the American experience and the romance of the American Dream.

But for the author's soul we must look elsewhere—in his own favorite among his novels, the one that cost him almost a decade of literary labor and private pain: *Tender Is the Night*. For its final title Fitzgerald chose a phrase from Keats's "Ode to a Nightingale":

Away! Away! for I will fly to thee
. . . on the viewless wings of Poesy
Though the dull brain perplexes and retards:
Already with thee! tender is the night . . .

The title evokes the transient, bittersweet, and ultimately tragic nature of Fitzgerald's "Romance" (as he had originally subtitled the book). By the time the novel was finally published in 1934, Fitzgerald had lost his own personal battle to save his wife Zelda from her mental illness and their marriage from the inevitable consequences.

The novel is as much a product of the author's own experience of struggle and heartbreak as it is his credo in fidelity, perseverance, and romantic love. It will always be one of his most beloved works because it rings true, because it is true.

But the novel was initially conceived in a very different spirit, back in 1925, when Scott and Zelda were still basking in the Riviera sun and the future was colored in Mediterranean hues. There, following the publication of *The Great Gatsby*, in the idyllic company of Sara and Gerald Murphy (to whom the book is dedicated), Fitzgerald planned a far more ambitious novel, "something really new in form, idea, structure—the model for the age that Joyce and Stein are searching for, that Conrad didn't find."

In the meantime, disappointed by the modest sales of *Gatsby*, he turned out a spate of short stories to support himself in the luxurious expatriate manner to which he had grown accustomed. Those days at La Garoupe beach and evenings at the Murphys' Villa America were perhaps the closest Scott and Zelda ever came to paradise, and the ambience is captured in the opening chapters of *Tender Is the Night*, in which Nicole and Dick Diver are endowed with the social magnetism and unique charm of Sara and Gerald presiding over a season of memorable fetes. One of the earliest references to the new novel in progress is an amusing afterthought in a letter of July 1925 to Max Perkins: "The novel has begun. I'd rather tell you nothing about it quite yet. No news. We had a great time in Antibes and got very brown and healthy. In case you don't place it, it's the peninsula between Cannes and Nice on the Riviera where Napoleon landed on his return from Elba."

Then, in October, Perkins received one of many prophecies reflecting the author's less-than-guarded optimism: "The novel is going to be great." In December, from cold Paris:

> *I write to you from the depths of one of my unholy depressions. The book is wonderful—I honestly think that when it's*

> *published, I shall be the best American novelist (which isn't saying a lot) but the end seems far away. When it's finished, I'm coming home for a while anyhow though the thought revolts me as much as the thought of remaining in France. . . . My work is the only thing that makes me happy—except to be a little tight—and for those two indulgences I pay a big price in mental and physical hangovers. . . . My novel should be finished next fall.*

The following February, he made an unusual request of Perkins: "In regard to my novel. Will you ask somebody what is done if one American murders another in France. Would an American marshal come over for him? From his state of residence? Who would hold him meanwhile—the consul or the French police? Why isn't that so if one Italian kills another Italian in America? It's important that I find this out and I can't seem to. In a certain sense my plot is not unlike Dreiser's in *An American Tragedy*. At first this worried me but now it doesn't, for our minds are so different." Perkins consulted a lawyer, who replied that the American would be treated like any Frenchman apprehended by the French police and tried in the French courts. "I hope this fact won't upset some plan you had for the novel," added Perkins, who was duly thanked for the legal advice.

"My book is wonderful," Fitzgerald wrote again in May 1926. "I don't expect to be interrupted again. I expect to reach New York about December 10th with the manuscript under my arm." But it was only toward the end of 1928, two and a half years later, that Perkins had at last read two chapters and commented, "About the first, we fully agree. It is excellent. The second I think contains some of the best writing you have ever done—some lovely scenes, and impressions briefly and beautifully conveyed. . . . I think this is a wonderfully promising start-off. Send on others as soon as you can." By June of the following year, in Cannes, Fitzgerald was "working day and night" on the novel, "from a new angle that I think will solve previous difficulties." Meanwhile, Zelda's condition was deteriorating so rapidly that she had to be hospitalized in a sanitarium on Lake Geneva. Fitzgerald wrote to Perkins in September 1930, "This illness has cost me a fortune. . . . The biggest man in Switzerland gave all his time to her and saved her reason by a split second."

The emotional cost would yield Book Two, the multifaceted character Dr. Richard Diver, and the Swiss backdrop for the psychiatric drama of Diver's ill-starred romance with his patient/wife, Nicole. Fitzgerald eventually went so far as to graph on a sheet of paper the parallel psychiatric "histories" of Nicole and Zelda, ending with two poignant question marks pointing to the future. But the immediate future seemed bright enough. Zelda had been pronounced cured, and in the fall of 1931 the Fitzgeralds returned on the *Aquitania* and settled in Montgomery, Alabama.

Work on the novel was soon interrupted by Fitzgerald's trip to Hollywood to work for MGM. In January 1932, a month before moving to Baltimore, Fitzgerald wrote to Perkins that "at last for the first time in two years and a half I am going to spend five consecutive months on my novel. . . . Don't tell Ernest or anyone—let them think what they want; you're the only one who's ever consistently felt faith in me anyhow." By August it was "plotted and planned, never more to be permanently interrupted." A month and a year later, "the novel has gone ahead faster than I thought." The draft was soon completed. "I will appear in person carrying the manuscript and wearing a spiked helmet. . . . Please do not have a band as I do not care for music."

Having finished at last, Fitzgerald admonished the ever-patient Max, "Be careful in saying it's my first book in seven years not to imply that it contains seven years' work. People would expect too much in bulk and scope. This novel, my fourth, completes my story of the boom years. It might be wise to accentuate the fact that it does not deal with the Depression. Don't accentuate that it deals with Americans abroad—there's been too much trash under that banner. No exclamation 'At last, the long awaited etc.' That merely creates the 'Oh yeah' mood in people."

The novel was first to be serialized in four installments in *Scribner's Magazine*, originally titled *Richard Diver, a Romance*. Fitzgerald himself undertook the cuts required for the serialization, though with considerable apprehension that they would weaken the story's structure, already fragile, and that reviewers would fault it without later reading the published book. He had equal concerns about how the novel was to be presented to the public: "Don't forget my suggestion that the jacket flap should carry an implication that though the book starts in a lyrical way, heavy drama will presently develop." Apropos of advertising, he added, "Please do not use the phrase 'Riviera' or 'gay resorts.' Not only does it sound like the triviality of which I am so often accused, but also the Riviera has been thoroughly exploited by E. Phillips Oppenheim and a whole generation of writers and its very mention invokes a feeling of unreality and unsubstantiality."

Among the early comments, one of the most favorable was by his fellow Scribners novelist Marjorie Kinnan Rawlings, who found it "disturbing, bitter, and beautiful. I am totally unable to analyze the almost overpowering effect that some of his passages create—some of them about quite trivial people and dealing with trivial situations. There is something terrifying about it when it happens, and the closest I can come to understanding it is to think that he does, successfully at such times, what I want to do, that is, visualizes people not in their immediate setting, from the human point of view—but in time and space—almost, you might say, with the divine detachment." Fitzgerald, still working on the proofs, was grateful for the praise but irked by "her calling my people trivial." She meant no slur, but the word hit a sensitive nerve.

The novel was published on April 12, 1934, to mixed reviews. But even the hostile critics acknowledged the magical power of Fitzgerald's prose. And the approving ones truly understood.

From John Peale Bishop: "You have shown us what we have waited so long and impatiently to see: that you are a true, a beautiful, and a tragic novelist."

The left-wing reviewers hated, of course, the self-indulgence of the expatriate characters. The Depression had intensified their antagonism to Fitzgerald. The reviewer for the *Communist Daily Worker* scolded the author, "Dear Mr. Fitzgerald, you can't hide from a hurricane under a beach umbrella." But these barbs were to be expected. The one that really hurt came from Hemingway, who charged his fellow writer with self-pity ("Forget your personal tragedy . . .") and with creating false composite characters in merging Sara and Gerald Murphy with Zelda and Scott, instead of inventing Nicole and Dick Diver from the imagination alone. The latter criticism elicited an impassioned apologia by Fitzgerald, an admirable literary defense that would have pleased his old Princeton professors:

> *Following this out a little farther, when does the proper and logical combination of extents, cause and effect, etc., end and the field of imagination begin? . . . Think of the case of the Renaissance artists, and of the Elizabethan dramatists, the first having to superimpose a medieval conception of science and archeology, etc., upon the Bible story; and, in the second, of Shakespeare's trying to interpret the results of his own observation of the life around him on the basis of Plutarch's* Lives *and Holinshed's* Chronicles. *There you must admit that the feat of building a monument out of three kinds of marble was brought off. You can accuse me justly of not having the power to bring it off, but a theory that it can't be done is highly questionable. I make this point with such persistence because such a conception, if you stick to it, might limit your own choice of materials. The idea can be reduced simply to: you can't say accurately that composite characterization hurt my book, but that it only hurt it for you.*

A year later, in sober hindsight, Fitzgerald did confess a basic flaw to Perkins: "If a mind is slowed up ever so little, it lives in the individual part of a book rather than in a book as a whole; memory is dulled. I would give anything if I hadn't had to write Part III of *Tender Is the Night* entirely on stimulant. If I had one more crack at it cold sober, I believe it might have made a great difference." But without the constant setbacks, the prolonged labor and pain, the bouts of "stimulant," it would never have emerged as the novel it is—the imperfect but authentic masterpiece that has deeply moved thousands of readers for almost a century.

The best appraisal of the essential value of the novel, the most illuminating "review" of all, is found in Fitzgerald's own inscription in a friend's copy of *Tender Is the Night*: "If you liked *The Great Gatsby*, for God's sake read this. *Gatsby* was a tour de force, but this is a confession of faith."

Chapter 4

Ernest Hemingway

"First: Last"

Ernest Hemingway's work first appeared on the Scribners list in 1926, a century ago. The Charles who presided at that auspicious debut was my great-grandfather, whose own father, the first Charles Scribner, had founded the firm in 1846.

In 1932, my grandfather—yet another Charles—took over the helm and, as Hemingway's contemporary, proceeded to combine the roles of publisher and intimate friend to a degree perhaps unprecedented in American letters. When my grandfather died at the age of sixty-two in 1952, the distraught author wrote to my grandmother, "Now my dear and good friend is gone and there is no one to confide in nor trust nor make rough jokes with and I feel so terribly about Charlie being gone that I can't write anymore." A week later, he sent an equally heartfelt letter to my father, who was once again on active duty in Washington as a naval lieutenant engaged in breaking enemy codes during the Korean War:

> *I won't try to write to you how much he meant to me as a friend and as a publisher. He was the best and closest friend that I had and it seems impossible that I will never have another letter from him. It does not do any good to talk about it and there is nothing to say that makes it any easier. Since he had to die at*

> *least he has gotten it over with. If there is anything practical I can do please let me know. . . . I will try and not worry you about finances nor about anything else. You don't have to write me letters nor have me on your mind in any way. I know what a terribly tough job you have now with Navy, Estate, and the House of Scribner to look after. They shouldn't do that to any human being. Please take it as easy as you can and feel free to call on me in any way that I can be of help. . . . This is not a good letter, Charlie. But I still feel too sad to write a good one. . . . Your friend, Ernest Hemingway*

With typical Papa precision, he then added this postscript: "Am sorry I don't know your rank so address this as a civilian. EH"

My father later commented on Hemingway's sympathy letter that he could "not imagine a kinder expression of condolence or a more delicate assurance of loyalty. And in the lovely phrase of Dickens, he was better than his word. For the next nine years of his life, he was as easy to work with as any author I have ever known."

When my dad first arrived at Scribners in 1946, following his discharge from the navy, he was immediately put in charge of advertising. He had to do everything on the fly: write ad copy, jacket flaps, catalogs, the works. His father and Max Perkins had given this neophyte a dicey Hemingway assignment in order to insulate themselves from Papa's expected ire. The problem was simple: Hemingway hated the illustrations in a new deluxe edition of *A Farewell to Arms*. Charles Junior would have to take the heat, as he was charged with asking the author to write an introduction to this edition, aptly timed following the conclusion of a second world war.

Hemingway's introduction contained a telling remark about his publisher, the man he called his "best friend." He wrote that my grandfather knew "a good deal about horses, as much as a man probably should be allowed to know about the publishing business, and, surprisingly, something about books." Hemingway thought of him not as a literary type—a man of letters—but as a horseman. This was key to the enduring friendship between author and publisher; it explains why my grandfather was the only one in the house who could make suggestions to Hemingway without being rebuffed. He was the only one who could persuade him to make changes, as he would do on the author's next novel, *Across the River and into the Trees*, which originally contained some highly offensive passages describing the character based on Hemingway's ex-wife Martha Gellhorn. Papa would listen to his friend and fellow sportsman as he would never to a literary professional, editor, or author with whom he felt in constant competition.

My grandfather and Hemingway had kept up a lively correspondence as intimate, colorful, and often outrageous as only two closest friends could maintain. Filled with teasing—what Hemingway called "joking rough"—their letters would surely be misunderstood by readers today, especially by literary scholars whose literalism exceeds their grasp of inside jokes.

I once received an advance proof of an article from a scholar seeking my permission to quote from family letters; she was convinced she had found in those letters the "smoking gun" that my grandfather and Martha Gellhorn had had an affair. The proof? A postscript from Hemingway saying, "Martha sends her love, whatever that means." Then there was a letter from my grandfather to Hemingway describing meeting Martha (by then the author's ex-wife of almost a decade) and her young adopted son at the airport and quoting Martha's jest that "she doesn't blame either of us" for the fact that she never gave birth to a child of her own. I could not convince the scholar that these were jokes; the only way I could get her to remove her offensive and ridiculous conclusion was to threaten to close our archives to future scholars and have Princeton explain that it was all her doing. It worked.

My father made a deliberate choice not to follow his father's example in his letters to Hemingway, who was a generation older. He thought it would be presumptuous. Instead, he decided to walk a fine line between seeming aloof and too familiar. "I knew," he later explained, "that Hemingway loved professionalism, whether in a writer or a bullfighter. He admired people who had a trade and stuck to it. That decided me: I would be a professional publisher." Yet in those letters there are glimmers of wit and warmth.

In one, my dad commented that at the age of eighteen months I had taken to pulling out all the books from the bottom shelves at home. Hemingway wrote back, "What young Charlie is doing is trying to remove all the dead wood from publishing; make a note of it for his biographers." On another occasion, my father wrote that he was concerned that I was becoming too citified (I still am) since I thought that "country" was just the word for my grandmother's house. On still another, "My children don't think I'm very smart. But I told them, how come if I'm as dumb as you think, that I'm making all the money for this family?" Hemingway wrote back, "That's what I'm going to tell my children." He, in turn, teased his young publisher (a new vestryman at St. Bartholomew's Church), "Charlie, I've been reading the *New Testament* and can't put it down: I can't wait to see how it ends."

Thrust into the presidency of Scribners at the ripe age of thirty, my dad was to be Hemingway's last publisher and personal editor. His relationship with our preeminent author was to prove no less fruitful (if more formal) than his father's had been. By the end of the 1950s, his last full decade, Hemingway was not faring well. He had suffered two almost fatal plane crashes in Africa six years earlier. Hemingway never fully recovered from those severe concussions. More recently, from 1959 to 1960, he had traveled to Spain to cover the rivalry of bullfighters Dominguín and his brother-in-law Ordóñez for a series of articles published in *Life* magazine as *The Dangerous Summer*.

In 1960, following Fidel Castro's takeover, Hemingway had to leave his beloved Finca Vigía, his home for the past twenty years. The new Cuban government then seized it. He never recovered from that loss either. Years of Homeric drinking, on top of a family history of depression, compounded now by diabetes, left him a shell of his old self in my father's eyes when Dad visited him at an apartment Hemingway was renting in New York City.

My father walked up Fifth Avenue with his editor Harry Brague to visit Papa and discuss the two books he was finishing: the first, his "Paris Sketches" (published posthumously as *A Moveable Feast*) and *The Dangerous Summer*. Both were virtually complete, but the latter needed major cutting: *Life* had just published less than half of its seventy-five thousand words. The "Paris book," as he called it, needed only some final polishing. Which one, Papa asked, should be published first? My father said the Paris book. But then after returning to the office, Brague second-guessed that advice and urged him to call Hemingway to find out whether he really wanted to do that.

Dad called and said that if Hemingway would prefer it the other way around, that would be equally okay. Hemingway went "into a tailspin." He had wanted decisiveness, not uncertainty. It was a serious error, my father realized too late, but fortunately not a fatal one. On the next visit, Hemingway asked his publisher to take a small suitcase to the office and lock it in his filing cabinet. It contained his will; he said, "Don't lose it." (They both surely recalled the disaster of his first wife, Hadley, losing a suitcase full of his early manuscripts in a Paris train station.) "If I lose it, I'll shoot myself," Dad replied. "That won't do me any good," Papa countered.

Later in life, my dad would recall, "I am bound to say that working with Hemingway was like being strapped in an electric chair. All the electrodes were always in place, and it would need just the flicking of a switch to ruin me. I might do something quite innocently that would be taken amiss and I would be in outer darkness forever. It was hard. It required constant diplomacy to keep everything smooth. I don't think it made me cowardly, but it made me nervous."

The next day, Hemingway arrived unannounced at his publisher's office; he needed to look up something in his valise, he explained. Dad knew immediately why he really came. He just wanted to make sure it was still there. After shuffling around the papers, he returned to my father's desk all smiles and sat down in his publisher's chair. Chair-less for the first time in his office, my father turned to play host.

"Would you like some coffee?"

"Yes, please."

"With cream?"

"Yes."

"How much?"

"Just enough to change the color."

Hemingway then added precise directions to the secretary for pouring the cream. "Only Hemingway," my father later recalled of this last visit with his most famous author, "would have thought out a specific formula for this commonplace operation. It was a kind of summary of his approach to life—accuracy, simplicity, and style."

A year later, after a repeat visit to the Mayo Clinic for depression, during which he was given a series of shock treatments and discharged prematurely (he tried to walk into the propeller of an idling plane), he flew back home to Ketchum, Idaho, and, a day and a half later, shot himself early in the morning while his wife Mary slept upstairs. It was Sunday, July 2, 1961. He was sixty-one. I'll never forget hearing the news on the radio that morning as my brothers and I played ball on the lawn at our New Jersey summer home. That moment remains as vivid as the schoolroom two years later when the announcement came over the loudspeaker that President John F. Kennedy had been shot.

That evening, I watched my father sit silently at the dining room table, writing in pencil on a yellow legal pad. It was his official tribute for the press release, with the time, 6:30 p.m., inscribed at the top of the page. I saw it again almost four decades later in a display case at Firestone Library in Princeton when my mother and I visited the Hemingway Centennial exhibition, which I had sponsored in memory of my father in the fall of 1999.

> *The magnitude of Ernest Hemingway's achievement as a creative artist has been recognized during his lifetime, and surely generations to come will agree with the judgment of his contemporaries. His books will always speak for themselves and will live on for centuries in that life beyond life to which every writer aspires. Speaking for Charles Scribner's Sons, and also personally, I can say that quite apart from the great privilege of having published all his works, the friendship and loyalty of Mr. Hemingway over a period of more than three decades constitute one of the brightest chapters in our history.*

After Hemingway's death, my father presided over the publication of the remaining works, beginning with *A Moveable Feast* and including the unfinished novels *Islands in the Stream* (for which he coined the title) and *The Garden of Eden*. His own account of these experiences with and without Hemingway is recorded in fascinating detail in his 1991 memoir *In the Company of Writers: A Life in Publishing*. It seems only fitting that of the four Charleses, he would be the one to assess Hemingway's significance as a writer and a man. The following excerpt from a lecture he gave at the Princeton Club Library in New York in 1985 seems to me as sound and sensitive an appraisal as any I have read:

> *Given all this professional scholarship, I am reconciled to preserving my own amateur standing and accordingly have decided to confine myself here to remarks about Hemingway which may seem obvious. Obviousness does not deter me. In fact, I believe that in this and many other fields of study, the obvious is nowadays neglected much too often.*
>
> *One of the obvious facts about Hemingway is that virtually all his life, from the time he was a boy to the day he died, he thought of himself as a writer—nothing else. That image of himself created his ambition, directed his will, supplied his greatest satisfaction.*

I think that from the start, there was a kind of enchantment about his commitment to writing. Robert Louis Stevenson, in his autobiographical essay "The Lantern Bearers," describes the excitement he felt as a boy when he and his comrades would meet after dark, each of them carrying a bull's-eye lantern under his topcoat. All the lanterns were lit but kept covered for the greater part of the expedition. Then, at the end, they were uncovered and allowed to shine out full strength. But for those boys roaming the streets of Edinburgh, the bliss in the adventure lay in the knowledge that the lanterns were lit and burning brightly even in the dark under their topcoats.

Like all true artists, Hemingway carried from the start a bull's-eye lantern under his topcoat. Most of the time, he kept it hidden from outsiders; he would talk about it tangentially, if at all. But it was there all the time, the most important thing in his life. . . .

Hemingway tried a number of experiments in the craft of fiction. One of his declared aims was to learn to write "one true sentence." The mini-stories that were privately published in the booklet in our time *were the first fruits of this effort. By stripping off virtually the entire context of an event and leaving a starkly isolated image in a timeless present, Hemingway found that the impact of the words on the reader could be greatly enhanced. Yet it is difficult to measure the success of that new style by means of the events that occur in that first series of sketches because the description of executions or horrors on the battlefield or in the bull ring are able by themselves to elicit strong visceral effects in the reader—regardless of style.*

But Hemingway did not stop there. He went on to apply the stripping technique to the mental states of individuals and to the relations between two or more characters. The stories "Up in Michigan" and "Cross-Country Snow" are early examples of the "subtractive" technique. The same principle dictated the use of laconic, allusive dialogue. The sparseness of detail forces the reader to pay close attention to whatever information is provided. As a result, the reader's imagination plays an active role, and the narrative thereby acquires the convincing force of something worked for and lived through.

Hemingway later used the technique to describe certain events of his boyhood for the clear purpose not so much of retelling as of reproducing the inner feeling of a character at a crucial moment in his life. To what extent Hemingway was influenced by Joyce's method of revealing similar "epiphanies" in Dubliners is difficult to establish. I believe that he was so influenced, but such perceptions can, of course, be neither proved nor disproved. The important element in Hemingway's writings derives from his constant concern to convey powerful psychological states: despair and hope, fear and courage, anger and resignation. Like Conrad, he was primarily concerned with the soul. The story may deal with the body, that is, exciting action and vivid sensations, but the ultimate goal is the transformation of character.

Several years ago, in discussing her husband with me, Mary Hemingway told me about his extraordinary ability to walk into a room full of strangers and instantly divine the multiple relations and attitudes within the group. It is that gift that was responsible for the psychological subtlety of his fiction, a quality that has been overlooked by many readers and critics who take at face value his reputation as a writer concerned primarily with external action.

Let me conclude by telling about an incident that occurred at Scribners. I was a young man at the time, attempting to earn my spurs as a publisher. It was not long after our publication of The Old Man and the Sea when one of our college travelers discovered an embryonic version of the story that had been published in Esquire in 1936. For all I know, the man may have been told about this by one of the English professors he had called on. That young man is now a prominent literary

> *agent—and what more can he desire from life? But it occurred to him that it would be an admirable thing to republish this* Ur-*version of* The Old Man and the Sea *together with the novella itself in a special college edition.*
>
> *We thought it was a pretty good idea, too, and proposed it to the author. But Hemingway—Hemingway the writer—did not think it was a good idea at all. Nor was he open to any such good ideas at any time thereafter. In the years that followed that episode, I often remembered Hemingway's fury at the suggestion. Why was he so put out? Until recently, I ascribed this to his well-known resentment of scholars who ferreted out his sources or explored his life. In these matters, he was apt to express the combined disbelief and despair of a magician when someone in the audience kept trying to explain his feats. Now, I think I have a sharper understanding of that annoyance many years ago. For Hemingway, his story had an outside and an inside. The outside might be the basis for a good yarn, and so it was in* Esquire. *But only the inside could be the basis for a work of literature.*

On publication of *The Old Man and the Sea* in the fall of 1952, Hemingway inscribed in his publisher's copy of the novella, "D'abord il faut durer": First of all, one must endure. My father later gave it the shortest imaginable translation—two words: "First: last." Hemingway still endures, and shall last, as the towering figure of twentieth-century American literature.

CHAPTER 5

Crying Wolfe

"Last Poem"

THE DESK HAD BELONGED TO THE LEGENDARY EDITOR MAXWELL Perkins. Before that, it had been used by my great-granduncle Arthur Scribner, youngest of the founder's sons. I inherited it the first day I began work at the publishing house because the senior editor with the best claim to it complained that it ran her stockings! That massive Victorian oak piece had occupied the southwest corner of our building at 597 Fifth Avenue ever since the company moved there in 1913. On it Perkins conducted his voluminous correspondence with his prize authors: Hemingway, Fitzgerald, Wolfe, and Rawlings. The desk was the scene of Hemingway's impromptu wrestling match with a fellow Scribner author, the left-wing critic Max Eastman. It was also the target of Fitzgerald's homburg, which Scott tossed over the glass-and-oak partition to announce his arrival. And it was the workbench for Perkins's most laborious undertaking: his Herculean editing and pruning of two massive—indeed, monstrous—manuscripts by our author Thomas Wolfe for his first two novels, *Look Homeward, Angel* and *Of Time and the River*. Perkins's relationship with Wolfe went far beyond that of editor to author. He was also Wolfe's confidant, champion, and surrogate father.

The biggest Scribner book ever edited by the great Max Perkins was Wolfe's second novel, *Of Time and the River*. The sprawling manuscript had arrived in crates and was originally conceived to require several volumes, à la Proust. The major surgery performed on it by Max Perkins was without question the most demanding labor of that editor's career at the desk. On one occasion, Wolfe, bruised by that operation in process, came into Max's office and spotted on the desk an ashtray fashioned in the shape of a coiled rattlesnake, given to Perkins by the Western writer Will James. Pointing to it, Wolfe solemnly announced, "Portrait of an editor."

Yet Wolfe prefaced his new novel with an over-the-top dedication suggesting that Max had played the critical (if not chief) role in its final form. He had so often said to others that he couldn't have written his books without Max.

By nature a shy and self-effacing man, Perkins was deeply embarrassed by Wolfe's hyperbolic tribute; indeed, he was to pay a bitter price for it when Wolfe soon after decided he had to prove—to himself, to the critics, and to the public—that he could write a book without Max.

After penning several stormy and reproachful letters, Wolfe left Perkins and Scribners. His last books were to be published by Harper & Brothers—posthumously, as it turned out—and with the final irony that Perkins, whom Wolfe had earlier appointed his literary executor, had to oversee their publication.

Perkins kept Wolfe's angry letters buried in his desk, where they were found years after his death. Evidently he could not bear to have his colleagues see the dark side of the author's personality. The desk was cleaned out several times after it passed to successive senior editors before I landed at it. All the original contents had found their way into our archives at Princeton—almost.

One day, irritated that a drawer would not close completely, I removed it to see what was blocking it. I reached into a half century of dust and found two crumpled sheets of paper clipped to a photograph. Not exactly buried treasure, or at least not at first sight. The battered photograph was of Thomas Wolfe, a photo of his portrait by Douglas Gorsline, with a note by Wolfe's agent, Elizabeth Nowell: "This is Max Perkins's only personal copy. Please be sure not to mark or deface it in any way." The accompanying sheets of paper were a typescript poem titled, in a very rough hand, "Last Poem," with "Brooklyn (1934)" inscribed below the title.

Oh, will you ever return to me,
my wild first force, will you return
When the old madness comes to
blacken in me and to burn
Slow in my brain like a slow fire
in a blackened brazier—dull
like a smear of blood,
Humid, and hot and evil, slow-sweltering
up in a flood! . . .

It took no Sherlock Holmes to deduce its authorship. Aside from the circumstantial evidence of desk and photo, the impassioned poetic voice and baroque imagery were as telltale as the frenzied handwriting. The next week I gave the poem its first public reading at a reception we were hosting, by pure coincidence, for the Thomas Wolfe Society in our editorial library, where Wolfe had spent many a night sleeping on the floor; he had wanted to read all his publisher's books, he explained. That literary giant did everything to excess, even once helping himself to a huge bowl of "stew" at my grandparents' house in Far Hills in the middle of a Homeric night of drinking with another houseguest. The next morning, my grandmother, who was raising a dozen show dogs—cairn terriers—heard the panicked cook scream from the kitchen, "What happened to all the dog food?"

After that ceremonial reading, I gave the poem to the Princeton University Library and then published it along with my tale in an early issue of the revived *Vanity Fair* in 1983. As Fitzgerald wrote, "If it wasn't life, it was magnificent." A few years later, Max's desk followed the poem to Princeton. It now rests in the university librarian's office, next to my father's treasured drawing room chair that once belonged to Sir Isaac Newton. Neither will be in danger of disappearing into a thrift shop through some oversight of future generations.

Chapter 6

Five Best Books on Family Businesses

I, Claudius (1934), by Robert Graves

Founding a family business for the ages? Think big. The Roman Empire, for starters, the subject of the classical historian and poet's perennial best seller: a fictional memoir by the most unlikely emperor of all, who recounts with wit and candor the course of that Julio-Claudian family business founded by his step-grandfather, Caesar Augustus. In forty years Augustus doubled the size of his empire. His family proved more outrageous, conniving, and deadly than the Sopranos. Next came Augustus's stepson Tiberius, followed by his great-nephew Caligula, the apotheosis of depravity. Caligula's uncle, the stuttering bookworm Claudius, survived to rule the business next since no one took him seriously enough to murder. "I am supposed to be an utter fool," he confesses, "and the more I read the more fool they think me." Following his sudden crowning by the guardsmen who had just dispatched Caligula, Claudius muses, "So, I'm Emperor, am I? What nonsense! But at least I'll be able to make people read my books now." His "confidential history," as he calls it, is a Horatian "monument more durable than bronze."

The Valley of Decision (1942), by Marcia Davenport

The author of the first American biography of Mozart (1932) and the best novel about opera, *Of Lena Geyer* (1936), never skimped on research: *Mozart* took her to Prague; *Lena Geyer* drew deep from her mother, Metropolitan Opera soprano Alma Gluck, who starred with Caruso. Marcia's unhappy first marriage found her in Pittsburgh for eighteen months, which inspired her most famous book, a family saga about the Pittsburgh industry that won two world wars: steel. It follows the Scott family through four generations of industrial growth, labor unrest, strikes, a world war, and the Depression. The protagonist of this riveting "upstairs/downstairs" drama is a young Irish maid, Mary Rafferty, who comes to work for the family as a sixteen-year-old. The son and heir, Paul, introduces her to the world of books, through which she loses her brogue and gains her place as the family's confidant and advisor—and "constant image" of the beloved. (Here a curtain must be drawn: no spoilers.) Marcia's time in Czechoslovakia yielded an authentic supporting cast of steelworkers. Asked decades later whether she would change anything, she replied, "Adverbs."

VANDERBILT: THE RISE AND FALL OF AN AMERICAN DYNASTY (2021), BY ANDERSON COOPER AND KATHERINE HOWE

CNN's Anderson Cooper first learned about his (and my) ancestor Cornelius "Commodore" Vanderbilt as a six-year-old seeing the tycoon's bronze statue outside Grand Central Station; he was the richest American at his death. In this spirited personal history, Anderson recalls, "I was convinced that all grandparents turned into statues when they died." A Dutch-American farm boy on Staten Island, Cornelius started with a rowboat and, through sheer force of will, built it into a ferry business that dominated New York Harbor. After the Supreme Court struck down the New York law that protected the steamboat monopoly, he turned to railroads. His lust for money stemmed not from the pleasures it could bestow or the social or political power it could buy but just from the thrill of making it. His son William doubled the family fortune. The next three generations would spend it with a vengeance—"the story of the greatest American fortune ever squandered." By the time the author's mother—heiress Gloria Vanderbilt—died, it was gone. Yet this engrossing tale is not without a redeeming irony. The Commodore was no philanthropist, but the widower's second wife persuaded him to make a singular donation: the founding of Vanderbilt University, his name writ large for the ages. As Winston Churchill noted, "You make a living by what you earn; you make a life by what you give."

Richard II (1597), by William Shakespeare

The English monarchy—dubbed "The Firm" by current royals—ranks high among ancient family businesses. But a "peaceful transfer of power" was not always the norm, as Shakespeare reminds us. Richard is a most eloquent CEO. The tragic young king insists he was "not born to sue, but to command"; yet, vain, foppish, and irresolute, he proves a born poet, not ruler. When his alpha male cousin Henry Bolingbroke arrives with an army to challenge him, Richard laments, "For God's sake let us sit upon the ground and tell sad stories of the death of kings." In soaring cadences he vacillates from insistence on his divine right ("show us the hand of God that hath dismissed us from our stewardship") to mythic resignation ("Down, down I come like glistering Phaeton wanting the manage of unruly jades"). Sir John Gielgud virtually sang the title role on stage: this tale of troublesome succession almost begs for an opera.

The Godfather (1969), by Mario Puzo

A family business need not be legal to thrive; in Puzo's epic novel, crime pays generational dividends. It's all in the Family—from Sicily to Long Island. "Italians have a little joke, that the world is so hard a man must have two fathers to look after him, and that's why they have godfathers." Again the question of succession is paramount. Don Corleone's golden son Michael, a Marine back from a world war, seems at first as unlikely as unwilling. His description conjures up F. Scott Fitzgerald more than ruthless capo: "He did not have the heavy, Cupid-shaped face of the other children. . . . His skin was a clear olive-brown that would have been called beautiful in a girl." (Picture young Al Pacino.) But he rises to the occasion—over several strewn bodies. This novel boasts more memorable—and useful—quotations than *Hamlet*: "I'll make him an offer he can't refuse" and "It's all personal, every bit of business." If *The Godfather* weren't fiction, it could be a handbook—too true to be good.

Old Masters

Chapter 7

Caravaggio

Shadows into Light

Caravaggio was controversial. In a "who's who" of painters, his police record would take first place. His antisocial behavior ranged from throwing a plate of artichokes at a waiter to killing a man on a tennis court. He was no less controversial in his art. Few painters in history have provoked such extremes of praise and condemnation from their contemporaries. No major religious painter had so many altarpieces rejected, only to be snatched up by some of the most discriminating connoisseurs of the day. Caravaggio was praised and damned for one and the same thing: his bold and often brutal naturalism, his revolutionary aim to paint the people and objects of the natural world as he saw them. Doing otherwise, he claimed in a rare statement about his art, would be but "bagatelles, child's play." He was admired in his time but begrudgingly, considered a useful reformer who restored naturalism to art, who brought it back down to earth after decades of flights of Mannerist fantasy, but at the same time a revolutionary who went too far.

"It is true that painters who strayed too far from nature needed someone to set them on the right path again—but how easy it is to fall into one extreme while fleeing from another." So wrote the seventeenth-century biographer and critic Gian Pietro Bellori; he labeled Caravaggio a mere *imitatore della natura*, an imitator of nature, who often "degenerates into low and vulgar forms." That bold genius broke into Italian art at the dawn of the Baroque like a bolt of lightning, electrifying his own age and sending a current through the art of the entire seventeenth century. He lived only thirty-nine years, his career confined to two decades and a few dozen major commissions. He had no workshop, no students or school of assistants, and yet he left an indelible imprint on artists to come, including Rubens, Rembrandt, and Velázquez.

His early years and training are shadowy. Born in Milan in late 1571, he was named, prophetically, Michelangelo; his father, Fermo Merisi, was a majordomo and builder (perhaps architect) for the marchese of Caravaggio, a small nearby town where the nobleman had his country estate. When young Michelangelo was five, the family moved back to Caravaggio to escape an outbreak of plague, but his father died a year later. Yet the family had property, so the boy probably had a standard education—Latin, catechism, math. Before he turned fourteen, he was apprenticed to Simone Peterzano in Milan for four years—an eminently forgettable painter who signed himself "pupil of Titian." Then the young man was back in Caravaggio for a few years.

Approaching his twenty-first birthday in 1592 with his share of an inheritance (his mother had died two years earlier), he set out for Rome—still the cultural capital of Europe and a mecca for aspiring artists—probably meeting up with his uncle, a priest in the papal city. A Vatican lawyer, Monsignor Pandolfo Pucci ("Monsignor Insalata"), housed him in exchange for turning out copies of devotional pictures to be shipped back to his hometown for sale.

The next year, Caravaggio teamed up with a young Sicilian painter, fifteen-year-old Mario Minniti (his companion and helper for several years to come), and turned out hack work for another Sicilian painter named Lorenzo, small pictures sold on the street or in Piazza Navona, as we still see today. Hospitalized for several weeks following a kick by a horse, he painted several pictures for the prior of the hospital. His first good break came in 1593–1594, when he was hired by Giuseppe Cesari (later known as the Cavaliere d'Arpino), a leading Mannerist painter of the day, to specialize in painting flowers. Caravaggio's *Boy with Flowers* (1593–1594) in Rome's Galleria Borghese illustrates his early proficiency in still life. His anatomy is less convincing.

From this time dates his first self-portrait as a pale, greenish Bacchus, the so-called *Bacchino malato*. After eight months with Cesari, Caravaggio found a well-connected patron, Monsignor Petrignani, a high-ranking Vatican official, and moved into his palace. For Petrignani, he painted *The Fortune Teller* (1595, Louvre) and *The Cardsharps* (1595, Kimbell Museum, Fort Worth), two multi-figured genre paintings, each a witty deception perhaps illustrating the misadventures of the Prodigal Son. *The Cardsharps* caught the eye of Cardinal del Monte, the Medici representative in Rome, who purchased it and in 1595 took Caravaggio into his palazzo near Piazza Navona.

The cardinal's sophisticated, rarified milieu is reflected in such works as the Met's *Concert* (1595) and the Hermitage's *Lute Player* (1595), both featuring music and androgyny (the lutenist was mistaken for a girl by Bellori), replete with symbolism beneath the sensual surface. The subsequent *Bacchus* (1596, Uffizi, Florence), with his un-godlike red cheeks and hands, dirty fingernails, and decaying fruit, and the earlier *Boy Bitten by a Lizard* (1594, National Gallery, London) have provoked various, complex interpretations—from homoerotic to moralizing genre with symbolic cherries and flowers of love ("no rose without thorns"). The crystal carafe reflects the artist's own studio window.

From the same period dates his earliest known religious work, *The Ecstasy of St. Francis* (1596, Wadsworth Athenaeum, Hartford), del Monte's patron saint, illumined by both natural (sunrise, campfire) and supernatural light. It represents an original interpretation of the traditional stigmatization of St. Francis: an internal—with no seraph in the sky—and intimate expression of a major Caravaggio theme that was to resonate eighty years later in the late Bernini. Caravaggio's *Penitent Magdalene* (1597, Galleria Doria-Pamphilj, Rome) could easily be mistaken for a contemporary genre scene but for the jar of ointment and pearls added by painting out a corner of her brocaded dress. We may compare her to his regal *St. Catherine* in Madrid, painted a year or two later, shown with the still life of martyrdom: the wheel, sword, palm, and faint halo that once again lift the image out of genre painting or portraiture. The darkening atmosphere already foreshadows his *Judith Beheading Holofernes* (1599, National Gallery, Rome), Caravaggio's first example of high drama and violence in a biblical scene, with a sword now wielded in deadly action.

Caravaggio recapitulated in the Assyrian Holofernes's "silent scream" his decapitated *Medusa* (1598, Uffizi), whose horrifying head had turned men to stone, here painted on a ceremonial shield given to Ferdinando de' Medici by Cardinal del Monte. The *Judith* marks a turning point, away from the softly lit pictures of profane pleasures to dramatic religious subjects illumined by metaphysical light. Since the beheading takes place in the dead of night, this light—too warm for a lightning flash—clearly emanates from some divine, supernatural source. The setting is minimal, while expansive gestures and heightened emotions permeate the canvas.

Caravaggio's brilliant masterpiece of this new mature style, *The Supper at Emmaus* (1601, National Gallery, London), is almost identical in dimensions and format, a tour de force of technique and innovation by the artist approaching thirty years of age. This is the painting that Bellori singled out for "failing in decorum." Bellori castigated "the rustic character of the two apostles, the Lord who is shown young and without a beard, the innkeeper's failure to remove his cap, and a basket of fruit out of season" (for a biblical scene that takes place the day after Easter, in springtime). Yet, three centuries later, the artist Frank Stella would write in the *New York Times*, "Abstraction today wants to make sure it can

Caravaggio, *The Supper at Emmaus* (1601, National Gallery, London)

have everything Caravaggio served up in *The Supper at Emmaus*, a painting filled with projective gesture, psychological presence, and pictorial import."

Caravaggio follows St. Luke's biblical account of the story and the Venetian tradition of depicting a scene of startled recognition at the moment when Christ blesses the bread—a variation on Leonardo's *Last Supper*. The resurrected Christ's far-reaching gesture is framed by the thunderstruck disciples, the right one flinging his arms in the form of a cross as though to exclaim, "But, Lord, you were crucified!" The Renaissance theorist Leon Battista Alberti wrote that the movements of the body reflect those of the soul, and therefore thought and feeling should be conveyed through outward gestures by artists. Already Caravaggio reveals himself as a master of psychological and dramatic rhetoric. His gestures speak louder than words.

But what of Bellori's complaints? Let's cross-examine them. First, the youthful and beardless Christ, so unlike the familiar face of Jesus. (Bernard Berenson called him "against all tradition and precedents, a boy preacher startling the yokels out of their wits.") Yet this face reveals Caravaggio's answer to the mystery of why these disciples had failed to recognize their risen lord—an original solution he based on scripture: St. Mark's brief reference (16:12) to the risen Christ appearing to his disciples "in another likeness." The particular likeness he chose harks back to the earliest type in Christian art—young and beardless—as found on the Junius Bassus sarcophagus and revived a millennium later by Caravaggio's namesake Michelangelo in his famous *Last Judgment*, which also reveals the source of Christ's contrapuntal gestures.

The innkeeper has failed to remove his cap in the presence of the Lord because he remains apart from this miraculous revelation, lit by metaphysical light, the light of enlightenment. But his head casts a symbolic shadow—a negative halo—above Christ's head, where we might otherwise expect the more traditional one, perhaps signifying that even those ignorant of Christ may yet honor him unconsciously. Likewise, the "out-of-season" basket of fruit is full of Eucharistic grapes, the apple of Adam's fall, and a pomegranate—symbol of resurrection. It recalls Caravaggio's early still life paintings like the Borghese *Boy with Fruit* and rivals his only pure surviving still life—that magnificent basket in Milan's Brera, a small but monumental masterpiece once owned by Cardinal Borromeo. Here at Emmaus, perched more precariously at the table's edge, the basket casts a shadow in the form of a fish, the ancient symbol for Christ. Such symbolic shadows reinforce the metaphysical nature of Caravaggio's chiaroscuro—the juxtaposition of light and dark—recalling the Latin maxim *Lux Umbra Dei* (light is the shadow of God).

The disciples are indeed rustic, simple folk, common humanity, realistically rendered but dignified in their humility. One wears the cockle shell, symbol of a pilgrim, as though to say, "We are all, even the lowliest of us, pilgrims on the way to Emmaus." Caravaggio was repeatedly criticized for populating his religious pictures with such ordinary people. A friend once remarked that he was sure Caravaggio would feel right at home on the New York subway!

By this time, the artist had executed his first large-scale ecclesiastical commission for two wall paintings for the Contarelli Chapel in San Luigi dei Francesi, near Piazza Navona. Devoted to the life of St. Matthew, these monumental murals were the first of their kind in Rome to be executed in oil on canvas rather than in fresco. Completed in 1600, they heralded the dawn of the Baroque in papal Rome. But unlike the sunny glory of Annibale Carracci's overhead revival of Michelangelo and Raphael in his ceiling at the Palazzo Farnese, Caravaggio's dawn is shrouded in shadow. Is it indoors or out? Light from the upper right (over a wall, it seems) yields some clues.

In this dim alley a group huddles around a table—like the cardsharps—but here counting not cards but money. Christ and St. Peter at the right, the only figures in ancient costume, turn in their steps as the Lord points and calls the tax collector Levi to a new life as his apostle Matthew with the simple command, "Follow me." Christ's gesture, once again lifted from Michelangelo—naked Adam's hand in reverse—reminds us of Christ's traditional epithet as the "New Adam" and that we witness nothing less than a new act of Creation. Matthew points to himself as if to ask, "Who, me?" while his avaricious colleagues, both young and old (one with spectacles), keep on counting. The two young dandies, right out of *The Cardsharps* and *The Fortune Teller*, mainstays of Caravaggio with their plumed hats and ever-present swords, look on, puzzled. The light that picks out Christ and this group is once again metaphysical—with no revealed source—emanating from outside the picture plane. Perhaps the window covered with oilskin is from Caravaggio's own studio in del Monte's palace (as earlier reflected in the carafe of the *Boy Bitten by a Lizard*).

On the opposite wall, Caravaggio painted the physical violence of Matthew's martyrdom, a scene of cacophony and confusion—indeed, it went through two revisions. We are first drawn to the scowling face of the nearly nude pagan executioner, his sword extracted from the thrust, with blood flowing from dying Matthew, as he prepares to deliver the coup de grâce, and then the horrified scream of the young acolyte who turns to flee; the divine light of Matthew's heavenly reward is personified by a cloud-supported angel with a palm branch; from the dark background, a self-portrait of the artist peers out toward the viewer with a conflicted expression as he turns and flees the scene.

Two years later, Caravaggio was commissioned to complete the chapel with an altarpiece of the evangelist Matthew penning his Gospel. The first version, destroyed in World War II, was rejected by the priests—and immediately purchased by the more discriminating Marchese Giustiniani—because the saint lacked "decorum." His bare foot protrudes over the altar toward the priest and worshippers; his plebeian face (a symbolic reference to Socrates) suggests an illiterate whose hand, writing Hebrew, is guided by an androgynous angel. It was too sophisticated for traditional taste: a "Socratized" Matthew proclaiming divine inspiration through divine ignorance ("The wisest man is the man who knows he knows nothing"—Socrates). The second version is more traditional, now revealing the same face as in the side paintings, taking dictation as the angel ticks off the generations of Christ's ancestors on his fingers: *uno*, *due*, *tre*.

In 1600, Caravaggio received his second memorial commission: two paintings for the Cerasi Chapel in Santa Maria del Popolo. The contract called him *egregius in urbe pictor* (the city's distinguished painter) and called for the martyrdom of St. Peter and the conversion of St. Paul—the two chief apostles to Rome, here shown prostrated on each side of the altar—a revision of Michelangelo's Pauline Chapel frescoes in the Vatican. St. Peter, the first pope, crucified upside down, turns toward the altar in heroic martyrdom for Christ. The prominent backside of the executioner and his dirty bare feet represent something no classical artist would have dared shove in the viewer's face.

Designed for the opposite wall, his first version of St. Paul's conversion on the road to Damascus revealed multifigured chaos amid blinding light with Christ's voice ("Saul, Saul, why dost thou persecute me?") embodied in a heavenly apparition as in Michelangelo's fresco. But Caravaggio discarded this version—now in the Odescalchi collection in Rome—for a revolutionary revision, an unprecedented closeup emphasizing the horse's hind quarter, right out of a Dürer print.

He edited out the traditional apparition of Christ (not mentioned in the Bible), relying on gesture and light alone to convey

Caravaggio, *The Conversion of Saint Paul* (1601, Santa Maria del Popolo, Rome)

the internal conversion. The symbolic source of this supernatural illumination is a radiant dove of the Holy Spirit frescoed on the chapel ceiling. Its actual source, as I discovered to my surprise one late afternoon, is the setting sun that briefly blazes with blinding intensity through the high transept window opposite the chapel.

One hostile critic called this painting an accident in a blacksmith's shop. Caravaggio's Saul, dressed as a Roman soldier who had persecuted the new Christians, lies prostrate. There is no celestial vision, only an uncomprehending groom (like the innkeeper at Emmaus). Saul's eyes are closed: Everything happens *within* as Saul is converted into Paul, the future apostle and saint. Other artists had shown his blinded eyes wide open; not Caravaggio. He took the Bible at its word, for in the book of Acts we read, "Saul got up from the ground, but when he opened his eyes, he could see nothing." So, while he was hearing the heavenly voice, his eyes must have been closed—simple, logical, faithful to scripture. His gesture is the sole sign of the saint's mental state.

My first introduction to this painting—my all-time favorite—was through a poem, "In Santa Maria del Popolo," by Thom Gunn, poet in residence during my freshman year at Princeton. (Gunn was himself a Caravaggesque figure of the leather-and-motorcycle set: A more typical poem is "The Unsettled Motorcyclist's Vision of His Death"!)

"O wily painter," Gunn asks, "limiting the scene / From a cacophony of dusty forms / To the one convulsion, what is it you mean / In that wide gesture of the lifting arms?" Then, at the end, he finds his answer in this "large gesture of solitary man / Resisting, by embracing, nothingness." Those outstretched arms—defensive, yet embracing—and the sensual vulnerability of the sprawled body (which even the horse respects with raised hoof) suggest the sublimated eroticism of a saint in ecstasy; they call to mind another poet, a seventeenth-century contemporary, John Donne: "Batter my heart, three-personed God, for you / As yet but knock, breathe, shine and seek to mend; / That I may rise and stand, o'erthrow me and bend / Your force to break, blow, burn, and make me new"—and then, at the end of the sonnet, "for I / Except you enthrall me, never shall be free, / Nor ever chaste, except you ravish me."

Paradoxically, at this very time of Caravaggio's deepening religious vision and his success as a painter almost exclusively of large-scale sacred works, his personal life darkened. His name began to appear regularly in the police blotter; he was arrested fourteen times and jailed six or seven times over the next six years—for carrying his sword without a license, for spreading libel against the painter Baglione, for throwing stones at his ex-landlady's window, for hurling a plate at a waiter, and for assaults with his sword. By 1600, he seems to have moved out of Cardinal del Monte's palace—though on at least two of the times he was jailed he sent for help from the cardinal, and he was always bailed out by eminent friends, including the French ambassador. At the same time, his companion Mario Minniti got married and moved back to Sicily.

Caravaggio was now on his own, something of a drifter. Five years later, he reportedly had no permanent address. Though well paid for his altarpieces, which he delivered on time, he wore his rich clothes into rags and ate his meals on a wooden board covered with an old canvas as a tablecloth. Between work he paraded around the streets, from tavern to tennis court, brandishing his sword and dagger, followed by a boy—Cecco, his assistant and occasional model, who later became a fine Caravaggesque painter in his own right—and sometimes by a black dog named Raven, which, we are told, did amazing tricks. His rival Baglione described him as "superbo e satirico . . . un poco discolo"—haughty, satirical, and rather wild. Cardinal del Monte conceded that he was *stravagantassimo*—most eccentric. Perhaps that's the closest we can come to comprehending this complex, hot-blooded genius.

We may glimpse that proud, satiric side of the artist who railed against venerating past masters—he insisted that nature was teacher enough—in two provocative revisions of Michelangelo. The first is the young *John the Baptist* (1602, Capitoline Museum, Rome), stripped of all religious symbols (and all clothing) except for a sacrificial ram—an ambiguous quotation of Michelangelo's *ignudo* on the Sistine ceiling: "tra il devoto et profano," as one priest complained at the time, "between pious and profane." We may compare him with the more mature *John the Baptist*, a few years later, today in Kansas City, my favorite Caravaggio in America: a brooding adolescent already suggesting in his smoldering countenance (familiar to any parent of a teenager) the future fire-and-brimstone prophet.

The second, even more pointedly provocative, is his *Victorious Amor* (as in "love conquers all") in Berlin, Caravaggio's irreverent one-upmanship on Michelangelo's idealized *Victory* in Florence. Triumphant Cupid, an impudent urchin with bird's wings, brandishes his arrow as he poses with battle trophies of civilization and worldly powers. According to one account, this picture—Giustiniani's favorite—was so admired that it gained Caravaggio's release from prison. Arrests and imprisonments notwithstanding, the commissions continued.

Among his most acclaimed is the masterpiece of the Vatican Museums, his *Entombment of Christ*, commissioned in 1602 for the Chapel of the Pietà in the church of Santa Maria in Vallicella. Echoes of Raphael's *Entombment* (1527, Galleria Borghese) and Michelangelo's famous Vatican *Pietà* are incorporated within a triangle of grief—the Virgin here shown old, her protective gesture juxtaposed with those of the two younger Marys. The choreographed gestures and bodies combine in a diagonal descent, from right to left, from vertical to horizontal. St. John's hand presses the side wound as the body is lowered into its grave—the altar and chapel where the priest and viewers stand. The protruding corner of the symbolic stone (Christ as "cornerstone") connects the two spaces and realms. If only one picture could be saved in the Vatican, this would be my choice. His most acclaimed work in its time, it was later copied down the centuries by artists from Rubens to Cézanne.

The last of Caravaggio's Roman altarpieces still in situ is the *Madonna di Loreto* in Sant'Agostino (1604). These two pilgrims with dirty feet—"everymen," as it were—kneel in pure faith and humility before a vision of Madonna and child at the entrance to her Holy House in Loreto (transported miraculously by air express from Nazareth to Italy several centuries earlier). The actual *Madonna di Loreto* is a votive statue; Caravaggio's statuesque figure, its effortless pose defying gravity, is here brought to life, like Pygmalion's statue, by love and humble faith. The folded hands *almost* touch the Christ child's feet, bringing the divine within the reach of mortals. He seems to have used the same dark beauty as his model for the large altarpiece of *Madonna and Child with St. Anne* (1605–1606, Galleria Borghese) painted for the Palafrenieri—papal grooms—and originally destined for Saint Peter's but later removed to their nearby church before they ultimately rejected it. (Was it the Christ child's nudity, the Virgin's décolleté, or the grooms' patron St. Anne's shriveled face?) It was then purchased by Cardinal Borghese, the pope's nephew, who may have encouraged the rejection for his own gain.

The model for the Virgin may have been the mysterious "Lena," described as Caravaggio's "woman who stands in the Piazza Navona," over whom he got into a violent brawl and chalked up yet another arrest. In this strange symbolic work illustrating the Catholic dogma of the Immaculate Conception (the Virgin's role as co-redeemer in triumphing over evil), she and her nude son together crush the serpent's head as her mother, St. Anne, looks on—a quietly evocative (if somewhat stilted) image of three generations, or the three ages of man.

Another contemplative masterpiece, an evocative image of old age also in the Galleria Borghese, is his great *St. Jerome*—translator of the Bible, theologian, and penitent saint, whose own "skull beneath the skin" compares with the "death's head" set before him as a memento mori. Once again, muted colors and somber atmosphere are charged with a dramatic splash of red—as in his last major Roman altarpiece and most famous rejection, *The Death of the Virgin* (1606, Louvre, Paris), commissioned for the Carmelite church of Santa Maria della Scala. The apostles gather around the dead mother of Christ, here shown miraculously young. She is barefoot, as are the apostles—a source of contemporary criticism but befitting a church of *barefoot* Carmelite monks. Her bright red dress is accentuated above by the weighty bed hangings, suggesting a cloth of honor, a funeral dirge of fabric. Her face alone is bathed in soft light, while a faint gold halo sets her apart from the rest of humanity—the grieving apostles, a magnificent series of variations on a mournful theme, joined by the weeping Magdalene in the foreground: There she sits, spent, with head bowed before the copper pan of water and cloth with which she ministered to her savior's dying mother. John, the beloved disciple, is given the place of honor at Mary's head.

How unfair were the charges that Caravaggio had scandalized the faithful by displaying the swollen corpse of (some said) a prostitute. No doubt Mary appeared all too human and all too dead for some ecclesiastical tastes, but her poignant dignity is apparent to more sympathetic eyes. Indeed, Caravaggio's achievement did not go unrecognized by the young Flemish painter Peter Paul Rubens, who arranged for his patron, the Duke of Mantua, to purchase it—but only after a public viewing in Rome demanded by fellow artists. It later passed to kings Charles I of England and Louis XIV of France—not a bad provenance—before finally landing at the Louvre.

By the time of this vindication by Rubens, Caravaggio had fled Rome on May 31, 1606. Two days earlier, in a duel on a tennis court, the painter, himself badly wounded, had killed his opponent. Now a fugitive from justice—no doubt with help from some powerful friends—he had escaped to the Sabine Hill estates of the Colonna family. There he painted his second, tellingly somber and muted *Supper at Emmaus* (1606, Brera, Milan), an appropriate subject for the painter beginning his own long pilgrimage toward redemption—in his case, a papal pardon—for his crime. No more youthful Christ, no bombastic gestures: All is hushed as the more familiar bearded Lord reveals himself at a humble meal. The innkeeper is now accompanied by his wife, like those two pilgrims at Loreto. The lighting is dimmer, the colors subdued, the shadows deeper and swallowing the light. A melancholy air pervades the work, reminding us that the vision was but a fleeting one, that Christ would shortly disappear from their sight, leaving them to ponder his miraculous intervention along their journey.

Caravaggio's own journey would take him next to Naples. By autumn, he was at work on a huge altarpiece, *The Seven Acts of Mercy*, for the church of the Misericordia, an aristocratic foundation devoted to alleviating suffering in that disease-ridden, poverty-stricken city, the largest in Italy. The subject (or, rather, the *conflation* of subjects) is taken from the parable in Matthew's Gospel: "I was hungry and you fed me, thirsty and you gave me drink, a stranger and you took me in, naked and you clothed me, sick and you visited me, in prison and you came to me." To these six, a traditional seventh Catholic act is added: burying the dead—in the background, illuminated by a torch, an explicit and internal source of light new in Caravaggio but later so common among his followers, the *Caravaggisti*. Almost lost in the crowd is Jesus himself, dressed as a pilgrim wearing a symbolic cockle shell and welcomed by an innkeeper, illustrating Jesus's pronouncement, "Inasmuch as you have done it to one of the least of these my brethren, you did it to me." Above, breaking into this nocturnal street scene with metaphysical light, are the Madonna and Child borne aloft by a marvelous "brace of angels"—Caravaggio's most Baroque formulation of heavenly aerodynamics.

The following spring in 1607, Caravaggio completed a second Neapolitan altarpiece, *The Flagellation*, for the church of San Domenico. Set in a grim dungeon, with muted colors and dark shadows that devour anatomy and surrounding space, a sadistic triangle of torturers frame the suffering Christ, crowned with thorns, head bowed, being tied to the column for his scourging. He alone is bathed in celestial light, lending him an almost classical, statuesque dignity as he turns in dynamic and painful *contrapposto*. Caravaggio painted his next dungeon scene in Malta, where he had sailed in the summer of 1607 in the hope of gaining a knighthood. His former master, now the Cavaliere d'Arpino, and his nemesis and inferior imitator Baglione had both been knighted for their art, and our master of brush and sword sought no less honor. His portrait of the *Maltese Grand Master* (1608, Louvre) gained him the coveted knighthood a year after his arrival on the fortress island.

For the pro-cathedral of St. John (patron saint of the Maltese knights) in La Valletta, Caravaggio painted the saint's murky and yet spotlit dungeon scene, the grim finale of the Baptist's life. The somber, subterranean space opens up around the clustered group of protagonists: the executioner about to sever the almost decapitated head with a knife, his sword lying on the ground, and the jailer pointing to the platter held by Salome to receive John's head. Only an old attendant woman reacts with due horror, clasping her head while in the background two prisoners, detached spectators, look on. This is the only painting Caravaggio signed. Where? In the drops of the Baptist's blood! ("All my sins are mortal," he was quoted as saying—a confession here writ in red.) Despite the horror, an airless silence permeates the scene. For this painting, Caravaggio was given a gold chain, two slaves, and other rewards a month after becoming a knight. But such honors failed to temper his impetuosity, and he soon landed in a dungeon himself after insulting a noble knight. He escaped down ropes in the dead of night and fled by boat to Sicily—no doubt with the tacit compliance of the grand master, as an escape from that fortress would otherwise have foiled a Houdini.

In Syracuse, he met up with his former companion Mario Minniti, who helped secure the commission to paint the *Burial of St. Lucy* for the church of Santa Lucia erected over her grave. The grieving figures recede even farther into cavernous, silent space as the pitiful Early Christian martyr lies stretched out, her throat cut, awaiting burial by two burly gravediggers who frame the saint. Even the presiding bishop is relegated to the background. The focal point—with a sole splash of color, again red—is a mournful young man, with hands clasped, like a young St. John at the foot of the cross. This final darkening and resonant spaciousness of the late Caravaggio was taken even further in his next major commission, in 1609, for the church of the Padri Crociferi in Messina.

The subject was appropriate to an order devoted to caring for the sick. Christ is shown, as in *The Calling of Saint Matthew*, with the outstretched arm lifted from Michelangelo's *Creation of Adam*, as he calls Lazarus to life from the grave. Lazarus appears suspended between death and life, the skull and the light, with outstretched arms like a crucifix—surely a reference to the *Crociferi*, or cross-bearing fathers, and also to the original crucifixion on which mankind's resurrection ultimately hangs. Caravaggio captures the dynamic tension between death and life, between the corruptible body and the divine spirit, between his darker nature and the light he sought, like one of Graham Greene's tortured characters, the "unlucky ones who believe." Caravaggio's late religious works share with the novelist a profound sense that the line between salvation and damnation is often faint and thin—and rarely drawn straight.

Before leaving Sicily for Naples, Caravaggio painted two touching nativities, one for Messina and the second for Palermo. (The latter was stolen in 1969.) Both stress the simple and stark humility—from the Latin word for earth, *humus*—of the Savior's birth in earthen tones. A sadness coupled with awe pervades the two, especially the second—despite the intrusive angel announcing God's glory in gesture and a banderole inscribed in Latin. Caravaggio's late revival of the traditional conflation of birth and death, of nativity and pietà, evokes Mary's poignant prescience of her newborn's fate.

Back in Naples, in October 1609, Caravaggio was badly beaten by his enemies (perhaps comrades of the offended knight from Malta). He had been expelled from the order a year earlier. His face was slashed and badly disfigured, but he recovered and remained in Naples for another nine months before receiving word that a complete pardon was forthcoming from the pope.

En route to Rome, he landed at Palo but was suddenly, for reasons unknown, imprisoned for two days while his boat sailed on to Porto Ercole with all his belongings. In furious desperation, he chased after it along the burning sand under the merciless July sun. Finally, Baglione records in his biography, "he came to a place where he was put to bed with a raging fever, and so," his rival concludes, "without the aid of God or man, in a few days he died, as miserably as he had lived." He was just months short of his thirty-ninth birthday.

Like his earliest paintings, Caravaggio's final work remains shrouded. One compelling candidate, along with the more recently discovered *Martyrdom of Saint Ursula* and *The Denial of Saint Peter*, may be the Borghese *David.*

Though dated by some scholars to 1606, it has more persuasively been relegated to his last year—a last testament. Whichever its date, it was surely a painted plea by the fugitive painter to Cardinal Borghese for a papal pardon by his uncle. Thus it offers a fitting, if paradoxical, work on which to conclude.

David stands holding in one hand the drawn sword with which he has severed the head of the defeated giant Goliath. Here we confront Caravaggio's last and most tragic self-portrait, held in David's extended left hand, as he gazes down at the head—with what? Regret? Pity? Compassion? A traditional prefiguration—as well as royal ancestor—of Christ, this young David, posed like a figure of Justice with sword and scales, recalls the Lord of the Last Judgment. How far we have come from the other Michelangelo's *David*, that proud embodiment of adolescent virility and virtue.

Caravaggio, *David* (1609–1610, Galleria Borghese, Rome)

Yet there is a final, far more profound and confessional link between our two Michelangelos: this gruesome self-portrait of Michelangelo Merisi da Caravaggio recalls Michelangelo Buonarroti's own late and tragic self-portrait on the flayed skin of the martyred St. Bartholomew in his Sistine Chapel *Last Judgment*. Perhaps Caravaggio, having paid a terrible temporal price for his dark side and unsheathed sword, could yet through his brush express a faint hope of finding, in that final judgment, absolution—and light.

CHAPTER 8

Rubens and Bernini

Artists Who Didn't Starve

I'VE NEVER REALLY BELIEVED IN ASTROLOGY, BUT I'M REMINDED of the horseshoe that the atomic physicist Niels Bohr hung over his door for good luck. When teased about it by fellow scientists, he admitted that he personally didn't believe in the superstition, but he had been assured that it worked whether you believed in it or not. So perhaps, after all, my Gemini star sign accounts for my double life or career. I describe myself as an art historian/publisher, and I'm never quite sure where to draw the slash. Perhaps it also accounts for my dual focus on the artists Peter Paul Rubens and Gianlorenzo Bernini. Like the Gemini twins, the demigods Castor and Pollux, they form an all-star pair, together marking the zenith of the age we call the Baroque.

As the premier proponents of the Catholic revival in art, both attracted key patronage from church and state, and both could convey their message more seductively than Calvin Klein without sacrificing style or quality. They were consummate impresarios who were happiest when orchestrating vast, multifaceted programs. Rubens once declared, "I confess that I am by natural instinct better fitted to execute very large works than small curiosities. Everyone according to his gifts. My talent is such that no undertaking, however vast in size or diversified in subject, has ever surpassed my courage." Brave words; they might as easily have been Bernini's, who, on his arrival at the court of Louis XIV, insisted to the French king and courtiers, "Let no one speak to me of little things."

To execute their vast commissions, both artists presided over huge studios of assistants and collaborators. Each established a school of followers, and each reigned supreme in his city. Four centuries later, Antwerp remains the city of Rubens, and, in Rome, Bernini's indelible stamp of genius appears as immutable as the ancient ruins. These men of unlimited vision, confidence, and talent were, at the same time, devout Catholics and devoted husbands and fathers. Both were energetic, life-loving, thoroughly balanced men who lived in total harmony with society and with themselves. They confound our modern notion of the struggling artist who pays dearly for exerting his genius.

Perhaps these very qualities detract from their popular appeal today. Our age prefers to locate genius in a tormented Michelangelo, a rebellious Caravaggio, or a reclusive Rembrandt. Hollywood has yet to project Rubens's or Bernini's lives onto the screen. Yet together they reveal the epic, heroic qualities of men who towered over their time and indeed over the entire history of art. The following review of their lives and masterworks represents but a brief digest of my two volumes on the artists published back-to-back in Abrams's Masters of Art series. They each define *maestro.*

Peter Paul Rubens is an artist's artist. Over the centuries Van Dyck, Watteau, Boucher, Fragonard, Reynolds, Gainsborough, Delacroix, and Renoir all paid him homage with their brushes, as did Cézanne and Matisse. Yet it was said of him, "Of all his talents, painting is the least." He was also a diplomat, a scholar and antiquarian, an amateur architect, and a shrewd businessman—a true Renaissance man. One visitor to his studio recalled seeing him at work on a painting "in the course of which he was read to from Tacitus while, at the same time, he dictated a letter. As we did not disturb him by talking, he began to speak with us, carrying on his painting without stopping, still being read to and going on with the dictation."

Rubens was born in 1577 to parents living in exile in Germany. After his father's death, returning to Antwerp, he received a solid, classical education before pursuing a life in art. In 1600, he set out for Italy. His arrival in Rome coincided with the dawn of the Baroque—a new naturalism in painting combined with a classical revival of the Renaissance. Employed by the Duke of Mantua, he received his first diplomatic assignment—a mission to Spain to present paintings to King Philip III along with a coach and six prize horses. Perhaps not coincidentally, Rubens painted the king's prime minister astride a white stallion in his first major equestrian portrait.

Back in Rome, Rubens took up his lifelong study of ancient art and philology. This budding antiquarian was to return to Antwerp with a sizable collection of Roman sculptures, reliefs, busts, and ancient coins. Just as his Roman reputation took off, he got word that his mother was gravely ill. He dashed off for home—arriving too late for her but in time for the signing of a truce with the Dutch, which promised an economic revival for war-torn Flanders. He still yearned for Italy. But, to their everlasting credit, the co-regents Albert and Isabella made him an offer too good to refuse. As the archdukes' new court painter, Rubens was exempted from all taxes, guild restrictions, and court duties. He could remain in Antwerp and organize his own studio.

Two weeks later, he married the nineteen-year-old Isabella Brant. He bought a property in town and built a magnificent Italianate villa with a classical garden. There, in his spacious studio, he produced an enormous number of altarpieces as well as mythologies, hunting scenes, portraits, and allegories with the help of his assistants. One visitor recalled seeing "a large hall which had no windows but was lighted through an opening in the ceiling. In this hall were a number of young painters, all at work on different pictures, for which Rubens had made the drawings in chalks indicating the tones here and there which he would afterwards finish himself. The work would then pass for a Rubens." Among his assistants was the precocious Anthony van Dyck.

When the English ambassador Sir Dudley Carleton offered Rubens a diamond necklace in exchange for a painting, he flatly refused. Instead, he sought to exchange a large group of his paintings for Carleton's "rare collection of antiquities." Rubens was an astute salesman: "The reason I would deal more willingly in pictures is clear: although they do not exceed their just price in the list, yet they cost me, so to speak, nothing. . . . I am not a prince, but one who lives by the work of his hands." Virtually overnight, Rubens became a preeminent collector. His bravura in business was as sure as his brushwork.

Rubens was soon engaged by the Spanish Infanta Isabella as her confidential agent in the clandestine maneuvers for peace between the two Netherlands, north and south. His widespread fame as the "painter of princes and prince of painters" granted him easy access to kings and their ministers, who often discussed matters of state while sitting for portraits. For the queen mother of France, Maria de' Medici, he painted his famous Medici Cycle now in the Louvre, twenty-four epic canvases that elevate Maria's lackluster reign to the stage of grand opera where mortals mingle with Olympian gods.

In the words of the American artist Washington Allston, "Rubens was a liar, a splendid liar, I grant you; and I would rather lie like Rubens than tell the truth in the poor, tame manner in which some painters do." The commissions continued to pour in.

Rubens's domestic life was soon shattered by the death of his wife: "Truly I have lost an excellent companion, whom one could love—indeed had to love—with good reason. . . . I think a journey would be advisable to take me away from the many things which necessarily renew my sorrow." With a heavy heart, Rubens embarked on a diplomatic odyssey. The English king's court favorite, the Duke of Buckingham, was angling to buy the artist's entire

Rubens, *Henry IV Receiving the Portrait of Maria de' Medici* (1622–1625, Louvre, Paris)

collection of antiquities. The ensuing negotiations offered a cover for diplomatic meetings to seek peace among England, Spain, and the Dutch. The Spanish king was aghast that such diplomacy had been entrusted to a mere *painter*. Yet Rubens persevered and set out for Madrid. While waiting for word from England, he painted copies of all the king's Titians, the glory of the Prado today. Looking over his shoulder was the young Diego Velázquez.

When Rubens was finally called to England, Philip IV gave him the title "Secretary of the King's Privy Council of the Netherlands" and a diamond ring in order to elevate the standing of his painter-envoy at the foreign court. Rubens would never eradicate the stigma attached to one who "lived by the work of his hands." Four years earlier, he had declared, "I regard the whole world as my country, and I believe that I should be very welcome everywhere." He now set out to justify that claim.

Despite the English king's desire for peace, Rubens had to negotiate his way through a byzantine maze of factions and foreign intrigues at court. He wrote, "I am very apprehensive as to the instability of the English temperament. Rarely, in fact, do these people persist in a resolution, but change from hour to hour, and always from bad to worse." Yet he prevailed. He was awarded an honorary degree from Cambridge, and on the eve of his departure King Charles threw a royal banquet, gave him a jeweled sword and a diamond ring, and knighted him—Sir Peter Paul.

Back in Antwerp, Rubens devoted himself to his "beloved profession" and to his new bride, Helena. He was a widower of fifty-three; she was a girl of sixteen. He confided, "I made up my mind to marry again, since I was not yet inclined to live the abstinent life of the celibate, thinking that if we must give the first place to continence, we may enjoy licit pleasures with thankfulness. I have taken a young wife of honest but middle-class family, although everyone tried to persuade me to make a court marriage. But I feared Pride, that inherent vice of the nobility, particularly in that sex, and that is why I chose one who would not blush to see me take my brushes in hand." Far from blushing, Helena inspired the most personal and poignant paintings of the rejuvenated master. The marriage was as fruitful as it was blissful. Their fifth child was born eight months after Rubens's death!

Rubens retired from diplomacy: "I made the decision to force myself to cut this golden knot of ambition, in order to recover my liberty . . . and I have never regretted this decision." Philip IV, in turn, knighted him—the only painter so honored by kings of both England and Spain. For the new governor of the Spanish Netherlands, the Archduke Ferdinand, he designed a series of triumphal arches and stages erected along the processional route through the streets of Antwerp. These ephemeral monuments of wood, sculpture, cutout figures, and paintings—a Cecil B. DeMille production—required an army of carpenters, sculptors, and painters, all working under Rubens's direction.

Rubens was now spending the summer months at his country estate, Het Steen. There he painted the most expansive and glowing landscapes of his career—poetic odes in oil to the natural order of creation, an Arcadian vision of man living in harmony with nature, canvases that alone would ensure his fame as a landscapist, if no other works survived.

Despite attacks of "gout" (arthritis), which increasingly prevented him from picking up a brush, he designed for Philip IV's hunting lodge wall-to-wall mythologies, over sixty scenes inspired by Ovid's *Metamorphoses*. Yet, in his definitive self-portrait, that late masterpiece today in Vienna, Rubens presents himself not as an artist but as a knight with his jeweled sword from Charles I: the self-confident and proud—if now aged and weary—Lord of Steen. Following an attack of gout, he died in May 1640. His will stipulated that his vast collection of drawings be kept intact in case any of his sons (or a future son-in-law) should choose a career in art. As fate would have it, none did.

Rubens's artistic legacy extended far beyond the Netherlands and transcended temporal bounds. His art proved as universal as the man himself. Painter, diplomat, impresario, scholar, antiquarian, architect, and humanist—Peter Paul Rubens embodied the Baroque fulfillment of the Renaissance man.

To complete our celestial Gemini, we must look south to the Italian maestro Gianlorenzo Bernini. He, too, was the impresario of his age, and Rome was his stage. Born twenty-one years after Rubens, in 1598, Gianlorenzo was a child prodigy. Like Mozart, he had a professional father for his teacher, who was to shine by reflected glory. When warned, "Watch out, the boy will surpass his

Rubens, *Self-Portrait* (1638–1640, Kunsthistorisches Museum, Vienna)

master," Papa Bernini replied, "Well, I don't mind, for in that case the loser wins." The pope predicted that the lad would become the "Michelangelo of our age."

His first sacred piece, *St. Lawrence* being roasted alive on a gridiron, was indeed a marble echo of Michelangelo's famous *Pietà*. Painstaking and true to life, young Bernini "placed his bare leg and thigh against a lighted brazier" and then sketched his anguished reflection in a mirror. Before he turned twenty-one, he carved the first of a series of magnificent life-size sculptures for the Villa

Bernini, *David* (1623–1624, Galleria Borghese, Rome)

Borghese. There, his *David* stands a split second away from hurling the stone at an invisible Goliath looming behind the viewer. The statue penetrates our space and charges it with dramatic energy. It is a milestone in the history of sculpture, marking the physical and psychological incorporation of the viewer. David's intense face is also Bernini's sole self-portrait in marble: the mirror was held by Cardinal Barberini, the future Pope Urban VIII.

On the day the new pope took office, he told the Bernini, "Your luck is great, *cavaliere*, to see Maffeo Barberini pope; but ours is much greater to have Cavaliere Bernini alive in our pontificate." *Cavaliere* because the twenty-four-year-old had already been knighted. Urban was to bestow on him commissions that would epitomize his triumphal restoration of Rome.

Eager as he was to make Bernini his Michelangelo, Urban instructed him to study painting. But his major commissions were decidedly three-dimensional. Above the papal altar and tomb of St. Peter, he erected his *Baldacchino*, a ceremonial canopy translated into a landmark ninety-five feet tall, as high as the Palazzo Farnese, or an eight-story modern building. Is it architecture or sculpture? Two centuries later, an American tourist called it a "huge uncouth structure that resembles nothing so much as a colossal four-post bedstead without the curtains." But the critical consensus at its completion (it took nine years) was decidedly favorable, then as now.

In each of the surrounding piers, Bernini designed a colossal saint in a niche. Almost three times life size, his *Longinus* is composed of five separate pieces of marble, a practice Michelangelo would have condemned as befitting a cobbler, not a sculptor. According to Michelangelo, a sculpture should be able to roll downhill without damage. Nothing could be further from Bernini's conception. Longinus's outstretched arms are thrust into the surrounding space while his spiritual conversion reverberates through convoluted drapery—Bernini's distinctive hallmark.

For his early patron, Cardinal Borghese, Bernini carved a true "speaking likeness." He sketched the cardinal while he moved about and conversed in order to capture the man behind the marble. (Bernini's invention of caricatures reveals—in a few sharp strokes—his genius in distilling the essence of identity.) Borghese was doubly pleased. Before he had finished carving, Bernini noticed a flaw in the marble. In two weeks he carved a copy, which he kept hidden behind a cloth during the unveiling of the original. The cardinal tried bravely to conceal his disappointment over the flaw. After prolonging the agony, Bernini suddenly unveiled the second version. Like his sculptural technique, his sense of drama was flawless.

Following Bernini's fiery affair with the wife of an assistant, the pope advised his scorched sculptor to settle down and marry. Bernini insisted that his statues would be his children. But in the end, he complied—and with typical results. His wife, Caterina, bore him eleven children over their thirty-seven years of marriage.

"Bernini was made for Rome, and Rome was made for him"—so proclaimed Urban VIII. In that city of fountains, Bernini left his signature writ in water. The first of these refreshing landmarks is the *Barcaccia* (old boat) in the Piazza di Spagna. It makes a virtue of necessity. The low water pressure did not permit spouts higher than ground level. So he designed a ship in the middle of a basin seemingly rising and falling with the sea, with water gushing from its cannons: "waters sweet that quench the fires of war," penned the poet-pope.

Outside Urban's family palace in the Piazza Barberini, Bernini's *Triton* arises and blows his conch as in Ovid's *Metamorphoses* to signal the end of the great flood and the restoration of order: "Wet bearded Triton set lip to the great shell, as Neptune ordered, sounding retreat, and all the lands and waters heard and obeyed." Amid the cacophony of Roman motor traffic, it still sounds a visual fanfare for the Barberini pope.

At his death, Urban left the papacy on the verge of bankruptcy. Such was the price of Rome's artistic glorification over the past two decades. It was said of the emperor Caesar Augustus that he found Rome brick and left it marble. We might say of Urban that he found Rome stone and left it . . . *Baroque*. As impresario of this extravagance, Bernini fell from grace with the stern and frugal new pope, Innocent X.

With no new papal commissions at hand, Bernini now turned to private patrons—and created his masterpiece *The Ecstasy of St. Teresa*, whose mystical experience he described in patently physical terms, an artistic consummation of the sensual and the spiritual that evoked mixed responses from the prudish Victorians. Yet the Roman clergy applauded his achievement, in which, according to his son Domenico, the maestro "conquered art."

Meanwhile, the hostile Innocent was finally brought around—by being tricked by his nephew-in-law into admiring Bernini's model for a fountain he had secretly designed "on spec" for the Piazza Navona. "This design cannot be by any other than Bernini," the pope bellowed, "and this is a trick of Prince Ludovisi, so that in spite of those who do not wish it, we will be forced to make use of Bernini; because whoever would not have his designs executed must be sure not to see them."

In defiance of gravity, Bernini raised a massive obelisk on a hollowed-out travertine mountain from which spring the four great rivers of the world. There was some grousing about its apparent instability. The irritated maestro arrived at the piazza, studied his fountain with feigned concern, and then ordered men to string ropes and secure the obelisk to the buildings at each side. Then he heaved a sigh of relief and departed smiling. We still marvel at the fountain that, for over three and a half centuries, has transformed the Piazza Navona into the center of paradise and an immovable feast *al fresco*.

The English diarist John Evelyn wrote that he had attended in Rome an opera for which "Bernini painted the scenes, cut the statues, invented the engines, composed the music, writ the comedy, and built the theatre." At his church of Sant'Andrea—Bernini's Baroque revision of the Pantheon—the saint's overhead flight, his heavenly ascent, charged the surrounding oval space with the miraculous intrusion of the transcendental. To Bernini, architecture was primarily a setting for his sculpture, and it had to conform to the classical ideal of human proportions.

Nowhere is this ideal clearer than in his famous colonnade at Saint Peter's. Crowned with ninety statues of apostles and saints, these freestanding columns, four deep, were conceived as the "embracing arms of Mother Church"—a concept that was as functional as it was symbolic. The piazza had to accommodate huge crowds of people receiving papal blessings dispensed alternatively from two distant windows. Bernini's giant oval fit both occasions—and still does.

Inside the church, he designed a sculptural finale in the apse, the *Cathedra Petri* (throne of St. Peter), where natural light materializes through stained alabaster into golden shafts and gilded stucco angels. Bernini converted an awkward window into a brilliant source of radiance (see frontispiece).

His work at Saint Peter's was punctuated by a summons to France by Louis XIV to design the new Louvre. The sixty-six-year-old Bernini stayed for six frustrating months. His grand design would never be built. France was not to be ruled from a Roman palazzo. Yet he left behind a magnificent portrait bust of the king, prepared by dozens of life sketches—pursuing the king into council meetings, even onto the tennis court—which he then discarded before tackling the brittle block of marble. He insisted that he wanted not to copy himself but to create an original. When the king's doctor complained that its face didn't look like Louis, Bernini retorted, "My king will last longer than yours."

Back in Rome, and now approaching seventy, he guaranteed Pope Alexander VII's immortality—not in a fountain this time but in an obelisk raised on the back of an elephant, a witty monument to the pope's intellect. Alexander's soul was in turn the subject of his papal tomb at Saint Peter's. From its symbolic door emerges a flying skeleton, Death, brandishing an hourglass—a gilded memento mori.

For the next pope, Clement IX, Bernini renovated and adorned the Ponte Sant'Angelo—then the main approach to Saint Peter's—with ten colossal angels. Two of these he carved himself. When the pope ordered them to be moved indoors to be spared exposure to the elements, Bernini then secretly carved one of the outdoor replacements himself.

Bernini, *Blessed Ludovica Albertoni* (1671–1674, San Francesco a Ripa, Rome)

The subject of death was confronted head-on in his late funeral monument to the *Blessed Ludovica Albertoni*, who is shown on the threshold of eternity, clutching her breast. In this visionary *Liebestod*, her ecstatic death throes reverberate through the tumultuous folds of her dress while white cherub heads float, like snowflakes, down soft streams of natural light from concealed windows.

With the deepening of Bernini's spiritual vision over the years, a scene of physical ecstasy modulated into an interior

Bernini, *Bust of the Savior* (1679–1680, San Sebastiano, Rome)

transfiguration—from body into soul. He approached his own death with no less artistry. According to his son Domenico, he worked up a final sculpture—his over-life-size *Bust of the Savior*—as the summation of his artistry. Only his "weakness of wrist" (he was over eighty) prevented it from embodying the "boldness of his idea." Long lost, this parting piece was finally rediscovered and authenticated in the early 2000s at the church of San Sebastiano on the Appian Way.

To the French king, Bernini had insisted, "Let no one speak to me of little things." Now, preparing to face God and account for his life, he said he would have to "deal with a Lord who, infinite and superlative in his attributes, would not be concerned to count in pennies."

At the foot of his deathbed, Bernini set up an altar with his painting of the crucified Christ. The fever, followed by an attack of apoplexy, lasted fifteen days. When paralysis struck his right arm, he declared, "It is only right that even before death that arm rest a little which worked so much in life." He had prearranged with his confessor a language of expressions and gestures in case, as it turned out, he lost the power of speech.

On November 28, 1680, just short of his eighty-second birthday, Bernini died. When his friend Queen Christina of Sweden asked Pope Innocent XI—the *eighth* pope Bernini had served—the value of the artist's estate and was told 400,000 scudi (an enormous sum), she replied, "I would be ashamed if he had served me and left so little."

But Bernini left to Rome and to the world a priceless legacy: the treasures he called his "children." No, Rubens and Bernini did not starve in their pursuit of art. But as a result, they—and their enlightened patrons—provided visual feasts that may never lose their freshness nor ever fail to satisfy.

Chapter 9

Rubens Meets Miami Vice

This is a tale of the greatest adventure of my life. I am still waiting for a sequel. We begin on the coast of northern Spain in the town of La Coruña, whence the Armada set sail four and a half centuries ago. Its Tower of Hercules—the oldest lighthouse in the world—is two thousand years old. On September 16, 1985, this was the site of the almost perfect crime. Picture the scene: broad daylight, a local museum, the very understaffed Museo de Belas Artes, only two people on duty, no real security. In walks a man wearing a trench coat and carrying a screwdriver. Now the crown jewels: two oil sketches by Peter Paul Rubens, prince of painters and painter of princes.

The two works, *Daedalus and the Minotaur* and *Aurora*, the Roman goddess of dawn (alternately identified as *Psyche*, goddess of the soul), are small panels, six by ten inches. Before the end of the day, the security guard makes his rounds and notices that they are gone. There are no fingerprints, no clues, no traces, nothing. The theft is reported to the International Foundation for Art Research (IFAR). Rubens paintings, like the Medici Cycle at the Louvre, are usually much larger and more difficult to steal. These are often not entirely by Rubens himself, who employed a workshop of assistants. But the two little gems from the La Coruña museum are 100 percent autograph originals.

Rubens, *Aurora/Psyche* (1636, Museo de Belas Artes, La Coruña)

Four months after the theft, in January 1986, the scene shifts 1,570 miles north to Stockholm. The National Museum is having an appraisal day. A local artist named Harald Lyth presents a little unframed oil sketch of *Daedalus and the Minotaur*, which the museum's curator, Görel Cavalli-Björkman, admires but assumes is a copy. Lyth leaves the painting with her. A week later, he phones to announce that the owner wants the work back so he can sell it. At this point, Cavalli-Björkman opens the great "Rubens Bible," Julius Held's *The Oil Sketches of Peter Paul Rubens*, and sees what looks like an identical oil sketch. But it belongs to the museum in La Coruña in Spain. She then calls the Prado in Madrid and verifies that it has indeed been stolen.

This situation presents a quandary. Under Swedish law, the museum does not have the right to hold on to the stolen painting. The curator returns it to Lyth and then contacts the police. Their investigation leads them to the new "owner," one Ramón Ramudo, a part-time chauffeur and office cleaner from La Coruña, who now lives in Stockholm. Ramudo concocts an incredible story that he bought the sketch, which he insists is a copy, for $30,000 from two South American office cleaners who had studied in Leningrad; they wanted the money to support guerrilla communist movements in South America. Furthermore, the painting is now at Sotheby's in New York.

Alerted by the Swedish police, Sotheby's ships the painting back to Sweden. Ramudo's passport reveals that he had been in Spain a week after the theft. A trial ensues; he is found guilty and sentenced to two years in prison. But four weeks later he appeals successfully when his lawyer argues that the sketch cannot be the stolen picture because its dimensions are five millimeters smaller than the published dimensions of the Spanish museum's work. So Ramudo is now the legal owner of the picture. Yet the curator and prosecutors have no doubt that it is the stolen picture. They appeal to the Supreme Court of Sweden.

When their case is heard, in January 1987, the curator Görel Cavalli-Björkman has a brilliant idea. She juxtaposes a transparency of the stolen painting in custody with a negative of the published illustration of the La Coruña painting and then, in a masterly display, she slides the one over the other. Perfect fit! The

Supreme Court overturns the appeal, the guilty verdict stands, and Ramudo is sentenced to two years in prison. Alas, Swedish law allows first-time felons convicted of nonviolent crimes six months to put their affairs in order before incarceration. Needless to say, Ramón Ramudo does not need six months to hightail it out of Sweden with the *Aurora* in his luggage. So only one picture is returned to Spain.

Fast-forward to April 25, 1991. US Customs Special Agent Dave D'Amato gets a call from "Stan," a confidential informer, who says that an Israeli-Mexican woman named Orly Beigel, who has dual passports, is offering a smuggled Rubens oil sketch called *Aurora* for sale. Picture, if you will, not Stan and Orly Beigel but Frank Sinatra and Jill St. John at the Miami Beach Fontainebleau in the 1967 detective film *Tony Rome*. You get the idea. Well, Dave D'Amato goes into high gear. In his first art case ever, he phones IFAR. Anna Kisluk, a staff member at the time, combs through the back issues of IFAR's *Stolen Art Alert*, and while she does not find a picture titled *Aurora*, she does find one titled *Dawn*—English for "Aurora." Thinking he's onto something, Dave D'Amato assembles a team. First, an older agent named Hank Blair, calling himself "Hank Thomas" for this case and posing as a representative for a would-be buyer, meets with Orly and two Nicaraguans, the Alvarez father-and-son team who have just smuggled the work into the United States and are representing its "owner" back in Nicaragua.

Orly wants to meet at the Ocean Grande Hotel in Miami's South Beach. At the meeting, Agent Hank sees the picture and makes mental notes. He reports to headquarters that the work is painted on a thin piece of wood and depicts a "fat lady sitting on a cloud holding a lamp." Close enough. An enterprising young special agent, Zach Mann, visits the library at the University of Miami, finds *Aurora* in Julius Held's book on the oil sketches of Peter Paul Rubens, verifies that the image is the one that Agent Blair has seen, and contacts Professor Held about flying down to

Miami to authenticate the sketch being offered for sale on the black market. It could, after all, be a copy or a forgery—in which case there would be no crime. There's no certainty that it is the stolen picture from Spain. They know only that it looks like the picture in Held's book.

A week later, I receive a call out of the blue from US Customs Special Agent Dave D'Amato. He wants me to fly down to Miami to take part in "an armed undercover operation to trap art thieves fencing a Rubens oil sketch stolen from a Spanish museum." (My eighty-five-year-old mentor Julius Held has "volunteered" me in his place, he explains.) So off I fly to Miami and play the role of "art adviser" to a would-be purchaser. I am accompanied to the seedy South Beach hotel, the "Ocean (not so) Grande," by Special Agent Hank Blair. His words to me going in will later provide a *Newsweek* quote of the week: "Since you're going to die anyway, you won't mind if we use you as a shield?" I shoot back, "I'm not sure I want to turn forty anyway" (that milestone birthday is just two weeks away).

In we go. I am given strict instructions: "Don't talk, just look at the picture, nod, shake your head, whatever. We'll get you out of there, and then we're going to blaze in with our armed agents, but we'll get you out first. Don't say a word. Don't talk to these people." Agent Hank is wearing a concealed wire and a bulletproof vest; I have neither. A hidden camera in his briefcase records it all. We are surrounded outside on the beach by a dozen armed agents. Inside, I have a captive audience, and I decide to host a seminar on Rubens; I haven't taught one in fifteen years. I am in heaven. The drama gets the better of me. The crooks present a manila envelope. Out comes the oil sketch *Aurora* wrapped in a red rag. I turn to the ringleader, Orly Beigel, and say, "This is no way to wrap a Rubens."

Then I begin lecturing them about the painting, the iconography, the style. (Is it really Aurora, the goddess of dawn, or—more likely—Psyche, the personification of the soul?) No question, it is the original stolen from La Coruña's museum. "This is the most beautiful Rubens oil sketch I've seen outside a museum. Where did you get it?" I ask Orly. Her instant reply: "Inheritance." Agent Hank is getting hot under the collar (I later learn that the agents on the beach listening in were none too pleased with my captive seminar). But they get me out, the agents swoop in, and arrests are made. Special Agent Zach Mann calls it "the picture-perfect takedown." I have been paid—in advance, on arrival at headquarters—$500 for the assignment. As the agent was peeling off ten crisp fifty-dollar bills, I asked, "You're Treasury Department. Shouldn't I get a check?" He replied, "Most of the people we do business with prefer cash."

A year later, I fly down to Miami to testify at the trial in federal court. On my arrival, the US attorney tells me there is a big problem. The defense has withdrawn their stipulation agreeing that the seized painting is the stolen original from Spain; they are now arguing that it is either a fake or a copy, in which case there is no crime. I now have to convince the jury that the seized picture is beyond doubt an original Rubens, the stolen art. If its authenticity is in any doubt, the defendants will walk.

By coincidence, I have just come off jury duty myself in New York the week before, so I know what jurors need to hear; they do not want eye-glazing technicalities. After a testy cross examination by the defense counsel, the judge asks the two best questions that will clinch the case. First, he wants to know how certain I am of the authenticity. I reply that I recognize the painting with more certainty than I would my own children. When he follows up and asks the basis of that certainty, what my methodology is, I look at the jury—which doesn't know Rubens from the deli sandwich—and reply, "It's exactly the same experience, Your Honor, that we all have when a stack of mail arrives, and we flip through it, and we see we have a letter from Mom. We haven't looked at the return address on the back, haven't opened the letter. How do we know? We recognize the handwriting on the envelope. It's as simple as that. I recognize Rubens's handwriting." The jurors nod.

The defendants are convicted; the painting is returned to Spain. Special Agent D'Amato is honored by the king of Spain. I get a "Yorktown Certificate" awarded by the Treasury Department. (After the presentation my six-year-old son is locked in a holding cell—for fun.) I live to see forty.

In 2002, I fly down to Miami for a reunion with my favorite special agents to film the BBC-Bravo documentary *The Rubens Robbers*, which—in a coincidence I still cannot fathom—airs and concludes just minutes before Julius Held's memorial service in 2003. As Einstein put it, "Coincidence is God's way of remaining anonymous." Four years later, Sky TV comes to my apartment to film a sequel, *Miami Sting*, for the Arts Channel. I prefer the first one: I was younger. Both are preserved on YouTube.

After two decades of giving art history lectures at the Met Museum, I decide to cap them with a recounting of the best Walter Mitty adventure of my lifetime, titled "Rubens Meets Miami Vice"—complete with video clips. I can't dream up an encore for that sold-out swan song.

Chapter 10

Michelangelo Revisited

If one individual, and only one, could be chosen to epitomize our notion of artistic genius, it would have to be Michelangelo Buonarroti. Not only does he personify the Renaissance man, but he also towers over the entire history of art, just as his youthful *David* has towered over Florentines and tourists alike for half a millennium.

"Since, in the end, civilisation depends upon man extending his powers of mind and spirit to the utmost, we must reckon the emergence of Michelangelo as one of the great events in the history of western man." So decreed Kenneth Clark, standing before the fifteen-foot *David* in his celebrated television series *Civilisation*. Who today would disagree? Even during the artist's own lifetime, he was deified as "the Divine Michelangelo" by his earliest biographer, the painter-historian Giorgio Vasari, as well as by that great autobiographer and egoist of all time, Benvenuto Cellini.

At the age of sixty, as Michelangelo prepared to tackle the *Last Judgment* in the Sistine Chapel, a full generation after he had transfigured its ceiling, he received a new and unprecedented title invented especially for him by Pope Paul III: "Chief Architect, Sculptor, and Painter to the Vatican Palace." Clearly the Holy Father had no desire to share with other patrons any part of his Renaissance man. Seventy-five years later, his successor and namesake, Paul V, was to prophesy that the ten-year-old Gianlorenzo Bernini would prove "the Michelangelo of his age"—the highest compliment there was.

Like Bernini, Michelangelo was without doubt a prodigy. Yet, unlike with the prodigies Bernini and Mozart, the source of his technical prowess has remained shrouded. Both Bernini and Mozart had professional fathers to instruct them from the time they could walk. Michelangelo's—too "patrician" to labor and too poor to provide any meaningful support—failed even to offer encouragement to the aspiring artist. "I sucked in chisels and hammers with my nurse's milk" is the only explanation Michelangelo was to offer in later years. As an infant, he had in fact been farmed out to a stonecutter's wife as his wet nurse. That forgotten sculptor who first taught young Michelangelo to carve in stone surely left his anonymous mark on the ages. As Henry Adams wrote, "A teacher affects eternity."

Michelangelo was destined to live an unusually long and productive life—eighty-nine years, almost a decade longer than Bernini and two generations beyond the normal expectancy for that time. Yet what if he had survived no more than Mozart's thirty-five years? He would still have left behind a catalog of masterpieces sufficient to guarantee his prominence in the annals of art. Among these we would find the Vatican *Pietà*, the *Bacchus*, the *David,* and most of the Sistine ceiling. The last would surely then be viewed as his "requiem," the masterpiece that, reluctantly undertaken, hastened the demise of its creator, who had protested in vain that he was "a sculptor, not a painter." (Happily for history, the implacable Pope Julius II was unconvinced.)

Vita brevis, ars longa. In Michelangelo's case, both life and art were long and of enduring significance. It is nigh impossible to overestimate the influence of Michelangelo on later artists. While writing my books on Rubens and Bernini, I found myself constantly invoking the name of Michelangelo, as did those artists themselves in both word and work. (A biographer of Rodin would say no less.) Annibale Carracci is said to have advised the young Bernini to study Michelangelo's *Last Judgment* for "a full two years" in order to master the representation of musculature. Indeed, Bernini's two earliest religious sculptures emulated and reincorporated Michelangelo's Vatican *Pietà* as, first, the martyred *St. Lawrence* and then the expiring *St. Sebastian*. His first full-scale statue for Cardinal Borghese, in turn, transposed Michelangelo's *Risen Christ* at Santa Maria sopra Minerva into *Aeneas*, the legendary founder of Rome.

Several years later, Pope Urban VIII, who wished to make Bernini "his Michelangelo," ordered the young sculptor to study painting as preparation for the commission to fresco the benediction loggia of Saint Peter's. In the end, despite Bernini's demonstrable proficiency with a brush, the job was given to Giovanni Lanfranco. Yet, in his major religious works, Bernini was to fuse painting and sculpture in a truly revolutionary manner; two popes later, Alexander VII gave him commissions that fulfilled his late career as an architect, just as Paul III had for Michelangelo, who finished Saint Peter's (but for Maderno's nave, a Baroque coda) and capped it with the world's most influential dome—a worthy successor and rival to Filippo Brunelleschi's in Florence. Its Baroque offspring punctuate the skyline of papal Rome while its soaring descendants—both sacred and secular—crown cities worldwide, from London's Saint Paul's to Washington's Capitol. Under the dome of Saint Peter's, Bernini was to fill Michelangelo's evocative void with his dynamic *Baldacchino*. Michelangelo did not live to see his dome constructed; its final design is the handiwork of his protégé Giacomo della Porta, who gave it a more elevated, tapering profile than the master had originally intended. No matter. I agree with Kenneth Clark: "We can go on admiring it, and think rather more of Della Porta."

"He was a good man, but did not know how to paint"—El Greco's appraisal of Michelangelo represents the dissenting minority. The founding fathers of the Baroque—Carracci, Caravaggio, and Rubens—owed Michelangelo an incalculable debt and paid him homage with their brushes. Poussin, Velázquez, and even Rembrandt may be cited among the beneficiaries of "the Homer of painting," as Sir Joshua Reynolds dubbed him. In his last discourse to his fellow academicians in 1790, Reynolds concluded, "I should desire that the last word which I should pronounce in this Academy, and from this place, might be the name of Michelangelo."

A few years earlier, Goethe confessed in his *Italian Journey* that he had become "so enthusiastic about Michelangelo that I have lost all my taste for Nature, since I cannot see her with the eye of genius that he did." Sir Thomas Lawrence supplied a more biblical explanation: "God gave the command to increase and multiply before the Fall, and Michelangelo's is the race that might have been."

Steeped as he was in Neoplatonic philosophy, which to the Renaissance mind was wholly compatible with Christianity, Michelangelo pictured mankind and divinity alike in idealized human form. "His people are a superior order of beings," concluded Reynolds. The epitome is, of course, Original Man himself, naked Adam, that reclining revision of a classical river god on the ceiling who reaches out, languidly, to receive from his creator the spark of a divine soul. Yet the artist's mind that gave immortal form to that perfected male was to remain conflicted and tormented, a soul yearning to escape the shackles of human flesh.

L'amor mi prende e la beltà mi lega (love seizes me and beauty binds me)—so Michelangelo described in verse, as in stone, his soul's struggle against its earthly chains. One is reminded of his unfinished marbles, those fleshly forms that barely emerge from the confines of stone. Surely no artist in history has bequeathed so many unfinished masterpieces. Yet, far from being discounted, those incomplete metamorphoses reveal, as no polished *Pietà* could ever illustrate, the lifelong psychic conflict that served as a catalyst for his unquenchable creativity. This metaphysical pain was the touchstone of Michelangelo's artistic growth. It was the process of creation, not the finely chiseled product, that engaged his fertile imagination.

One of the most exciting developments in Michelangelo studies has been the overwhelming impact of the cleaned Sistine ceiling frescoes (1980–1994) on our eyes and, no less, on our appreciation of the Renaissance master. After five centuries of grime, candle smoke, darkened varnish, and clumsy repainting were dissolved and wiped away by Vatican restorers, we could finally view the ceiling once again ablaze with color—no longer "through a glass darkly," in the words of St. Paul, but "face-to-face." The inevitable controversy prompted by so dramatic a revelation and radical reappraisal of a familiar classic was heated and often acrimonious, as assorted artists and restorers (but only a smattering of scholars) charged that the Vatican was "destroying" Michelangelo's masterpiece by overzealous cleaning.

I found myself a reluctant participant in the melee when I proposed that the Wethersfield Institute hold a conference in 1985 at the Met Museum and the Frick Collection on the restoration in progress. Among the group of passionate protestors was an officer of the National Society of Mural Painters (USA) and a prominent religious artist himself, Frank Mason, whose own work displayed a stylistic debt to the "old Michelangelo," that proponent of a dim, muted, sculpturesque chiaroscuro, not the brilliant colorist—as we now know—who already anticipated Pontormo and the neon hues of Mannerism. In an open letter to the pope, which he shared with me, Mason argued, "Irreparable damage is being done to the greatest religious work of art in Christendom." He concluded with this rhetorical flourish: "Just as the many glories of Venice are in danger of sinking beneath the waves, so do the many glories of the Sistine Ceiling now run the risk of disappearing forever beneath a tide of solvents, swabs, and unseeing hands."

In Italy, the painter Pietro Annigoni, whose own earthy palette and aesthetic was derived from the grime-permeated *ignudi* of the Sistine ceiling, carried the anti-restoration banner. It should be noted that the most vocal critics were those who had yet to visit the chapel in person and, at the Vatican's invitation, ascend the scaffold to study the restorations up close. Those who did, almost unanimously, left converted and in awe.

For some, seeing and believing may never be reconciled. But for most of us, this revelation was a felicitous one—regardless of the textbooks that had to be rewritten. Even the former communist mayor of Rome (and art historian) Giulio Carlo Argan was unstinting in his praise of the Vatican team. For the restorers, scientists, and curators, the project was truly a labor of love. I remember at the conclusion of our conference teasing the chief Vatican restorer, Gianluigi Colalucci, by reversing the charges and accusing him of taking far too much care and too many years to complete the job. Surely it could safely be done in half the time? (It was then estimated to take twelve years; it took fourteen.) "But don't you see," he replied with a wink, "we want to take as long as possible—we'll never have the chance again to savor, up close, each brushstroke of the divine Michelangelo!"

"Well," I said, "you'll find your next controversy when you reach the *Last Judgment* and have to decide whether to remove all those loin cloths added years later by Daniele da Volterra on papal orders." (His deep love of art notwithstanding, it was hard to imagine the reigning pope, John Paul II, undoing that "cover-up" by authorizing the return of Christ and his saints to their original, stark-naked glory.) Was Michelangelo destined to join Robert Mapplethorpe in a posthumous scandal? Time would tell.

The answer appeared in the *New York Times* six years later, in 1991. The headline read, "Vatican Restorers Are Ready for *Last Judgment*." The "gloomy dark blue and gray" would soon yield "a vast expanse of brilliant blue" (*lapis lazuli*). But what of the thirty-some cloths over the genitals?

Recent tests had shown that in several cases Volterra did not simply paint over the plaster but replaced the plaster and retouched it in true fresco, so that the colors merged with the original surface. In those cases, the restorers could not remove the additions. The Vatican, which was once roundly scolded that the "genitals and organs of those in ecstasy" were "more appropriate for the walls of a brothel," was spared a renewed debate over propriety.

In the *Last Judgment*, Michelangelo gave monumental witness to his lifelong devotion to that earlier Florentine giant, the poet Dante Alighieri, whose *Divina Commedia* provides the epic prologue to this terrible juxtaposition of eternal punishment and divine bliss. Conjured up in the midst of the Counter-Reformation, of the Catholic Church besieged and yet defiant, Michelangelo's apocalyptic vision was to have a recurrent impact on artists for centuries to come—from Rubens's tumultuous *Fall of the Damned* to Rodin's towering *Gates of Hell.*

Dies irae, dies illa, teste David cum Sybilla, solvet saeclum in favilla—day of wrath, that day of dread, as David and the Sybil said, will leave the world in ashes dead. As a powerful translation of that ancient hymn, the "Dies Irae," into another medium, its ultimate successor is, I submit, to be found not in the visual arts but in music—in the great *Manzoni Requiem* of Giuseppe Verdi. Perhaps now that the restorers' scaffolding has come down, some inspired impresario may stage—as a worthy successor to Franco Zeffirelli's 1970 film of Beethoven's *Missa Solemnis* at Saint Peter's—a performance of Verdi's late "sacred opera" against the backdrop of Michelangelo's heroic orchestrations of color and contour—the definitive *son et lumière* at the center of Catholic Christendom. That each masterpiece was the product of the artist's old age is miracle enough.

Chapter 11

Velázquez and Teresa

"God Among the Pots and Pans"

One of Diego Velázquez's most enigmatic religious paintings is also a *bodegón*, a secular representation of everyday life: the so-called *Christ in the House of Mary and Martha* (1618, National Gallery, London), wherein a foreground kitchen scene is fused—both formally and iconographically—with a background biblical subject from which the work derives its title and meaning.

Velázquez, *Christ in the House of Mary and Martha* (1618, National Gallery, London)

In the foreground, an old woman gently admonishes a young servant girl who is clearly unhappy about her kitchen duties as she sullenly prepares a meal. The convincing naturalism of this *bodegón*, combined with the formal, almost liturgical, arrangement of the prominent still life, recalls the artist's other masterpiece from that same year, *The Old Woman Frying Eggs* (1618, National Gallery of Scotland, Edinburgh).

In each canvas the vivid descriptions of the different surfaces and textures—the copper mortar, the peeled garlic, the fish, eggs, and earthenware jug—both solemnize and celebrate the tactile values of ordinary objects. The young servant, shown in the act of grinding garlic, recalls Velázquez's *Servant Girl* (c. 1620, National Gallery of Ireland, Beit Collection, Dublin).

A deeper connection between the two paintings came to light in the 1930s as the result of a thorough cleaning. In the upper-left background of the Beit canvas, a biblical scene is represented as if seen through an opening in the wall. That background subject is the Supper at Emmaus, wherein the resurrected Christ suddenly reveals himself to two unsuspecting disciples at table (Luke 24:30–31). The connection with the foreground scene is simple and straightforward: the servant girl, in the adjoining kitchen at the Emmaus inn, is unaware of the miracle taking place in the next room.

Her counterparts may be found throughout representations of that biblical subject in Italian and Netherlandish art: the servant or innkeeper who remains oblivious to the divine revelation in the midst of everyday life. The fact that Velázquez has chosen to give her the place of greater prominence in this painting reflects a northern Mannerist tradition, exploited by Pieter Aertsen, in which the biblical subject is relegated to an adjoining room in the background, seen through an opening in the wall, while the foreground is devoted to a colorful genre scene.

Velázquez followed this tradition—perhaps through an engraving or copy of Aertsen's 1552 *Christ with Mary and Martha*

(Museum Boijmans van Beuningen, Rotterdam). In the London canvas, Velázquez did more than adapt the northern Mannerist device to his early biblical *bodegón*. He exploited the compositional inversion to illuminate and underscore the meaning of the subject in a way that his Spanish contemporaries would not have failed to grasp. The point of his *Christ in the House of Mary and Martha*, as we shall see, depends on the precise iconographic relationship between foreground and background. Their vivid juxtaposition charges the *bodegón* both psychologically and theologically.

Mary and Martha were the sisters of Lazarus, whom Jesus raised from the dead. The Evangelist Luke tells of Christ's visit to their home in Bethany—and their contrasting ways of serving him:

> *Now it came to pass, as they went, that he entered into a certain town; and a certain woman named Martha received him into her house. And she had a sister called Mary, who, sitting also at the Lord's feet, heard his word. But Martha was busy about much serving. She stood and said, "Lord, hast thou no care that my sister hath left me alone to serve? Speak to her therefore, that she help me." And the Lord answering said to her, "Martha, Martha, thou art careful and art troubled about many things. But one thing is necessary. Mary hath chosen the best part, which shall not be taken away from her." (Luke 10: 38–42)*

Martha's story does not end here. A woman of faith, she chose to follow Jesus. It was she who summoned him to the aid of her brother Lazarus, who had fallen ill and (as yet unbeknownst to her) had died. Her faith resulted in the raising of Lazarus, the most dramatic miracle performed by Jesus.

Throughout the Middle Ages, however, scriptural commentators invoked the story of Mary and Martha as signifying the preeminence of the contemplative over the active life. Martha represented the laity devoted to a life of toil and labor; Mary stood for the contemplatives (nuns and monks alike) who removed themselves from worldly cares to worship Christ without distraction. The latter, according to the commentators, had chosen the higher calling.

By the sixteenth century, this traditional, hieratic separation of the active and contemplative lives underwent a profound revolution. In the north, Erasmus of Rotterdam challenged it with a phrase that rocked the ecclesiastical foundations of the already fragile medieval order: *Monachatus non est pietas*—wearing a monk's habit does not make one pious. Those foundations finally cracked when the Augustinian monk Martin Luther renounced his vows in a final break with Rome.

Yet the Protestants were not alone in their rejection of the typological exaltation of Mary at the expense of Martha. Within the Catholic Church there arose three Spanish champions of the faith, three towering reformers later canonized as saints who spearheaded the Catholic Reformation: Ignatius of Loyola, founder of the Jesuits, and two Carmelites, John of the Cross and Teresa of Ávila. In their crusading zeal, all three combined a deeply mystical spirituality with an indefatigable practicality. In their lives as in their writings, they reinterpreted the respective roles of Mary and Martha by coordinating them with equal emphasis on the active and meditative aspects of Christian spirituality.

It is against this Counter-Reformation backdrop—both Spanish and Roman—that Velázquez's original reinterpretation of the biblical subject must be understood, for the key to its meaning lies in the celebrated writings of Teresa—or "La Santa," as she came to be popularly called even before her official canonization in 1622, four years after this painting. St. Teresa explains in her own writings how the gentle admonition to work—illustrated in the foreground—can be viewed as consonant with Christ's famous biblical exchange with Martha in the background.

That Velázquez intended such a thematic parallel is underscored by his repetition of costume: the white headdress worn by both Martha and the old woman, together with their rhetorical gestures of raised right hands. The further repetition of the pottery jug in both scenes serves as a symbolic footnote signifying that the foreground represents an amplified gloss on the biblical background.

In the course of her travels among her newly reformed convents, Teresa often found the nuns unwilling—like Velázquez's servant girl—to undertake joyfully the humbler tasks in convent life such as working in the kitchen. Her classic admonition, recorded in her autobiography (*Vida*, chapter XXII), invokes both Mary and Martha in a most original and telling context: "The first thing I would say is that it is a little lack of humility to desire to raise one's soul to heaven before the Lord raises it . . . to desire to be Mary before one has labored with Martha."

It is Teresa's characteristic insistence on humility and obedience that Velázquez evokes in the older woman admonishing the younger. For both Teresa and Velázquez, the ultimate point of the Mary-and-Martha allusion was essentially encouraging, as it recalls another, far more famous saying of Teresa from her *Book of the Foundations* (chapter V): "But my daughters, good heavens! Do not be disconsolate when obedience leads you to be concerned with external, worldly matters; understand that if your task is in the kitchen, the Lord walks among the pots and pans, helping you in all things spiritual and temporal."

Entre los pucheros anda el Señor—the Lord walks among the pots and pans. That saying of Teresa's soon became common currency in Spain, where it still remains a popular proverb with obvious application to daily life. It was Velázquez who first translated the proverb into paint. In his vivid gloss on the biblical story of Mary and Martha, he offered nothing less than a visual parable of the virtue of humility and the holiness of ordinary labor.

St. Teresa would have concurred wholeheartedly with this conjoining of the active and the contemplative in the sacred art of daily living: *Entre los pucheros anda el Señor*—with Martha as with Mary.

Chapter 12

Transfigurations

The Late Bernini

Over the past years, renewed attention has focused on the question of "late styles" among artists—especially Titian, Rembrandt, Picasso, and Bernini. In Bernini's case, the very existence of an *Alterstil*—namely, the expressive spiritualization that Rudolph Wittkower described in the sculptor's last works—has been challenged, if not dismissed altogether. According to one revisionist theory, the notion of his highly intensified and spiritualized late style is the result of art historians having "adopted unwittingly" literary conventions, or *topoi*, employed by Bernini's earliest biographers, his son Domenico and the Florentine academician Filippo Baldinucci. Yet, as Julius Held cautioned, behind *topoi* may lie historical truth. Indeed, however formulaic the Baroque prose, those two synoptic accounts of Bernini's burning autumnal piety find ample corroboration in other contemporary sources.

I prefer to turn to the primary documents—the ones writ in marble—to clarify the almost mystically transfigured contours and sacramental integration in Bernini's last works. His entire oeuvre, to be sure, reveals an extraordinary cohesiveness, a seamless fabric of innovation and recapitulation. Bernini's late style consequently reflects not a break or departure, but rather a series of revisions and resolutions, of sculptural transfigurations that are as spiritually resonant as they are visually dazzling. "If you want to see what a man can do," Bernini maintained, "you must give him a problem." The central challenge he tackled anew was the charging of sculpture with a metaphysical meaning, or *concetto*, that electrifies its surrounding space as it engages the viewer both physically and psychologically.

Bernini's sculptural projection of narrative through space harks back to his youthful *David* of 1623–1624 (Galleria Borghese, Rome), who takes aim at an imaginary Goliath looming behind the viewer. A few years later, at the crossing of Saint Peter's beneath Michelangelo's dome, he planned four marble saints-in-niches, originally paired diagonally to respond, contrapuntally, to Christ's sacrifice and resurrection symbolized in the soaring bronze *Baldacchino*. Three decades later, in the mid-1650s, he transfigured Raphael's Chigi Chapel of Santa Maria del Popolo with his diagonally—and now biblically—paired statues of *Daniel* and *Habakkuk*; their dramatic relation bisects the domed Renaissance space along a spiritually charged axis, fulfilling Bernini's original plan for the crossing of Saint Peter's.

In the 1660s, at Sant'Andrea al Quirinale, through his *bel composto* (or beautiful blending) of architecture, sculpture, and painting, he similarly exploited a narrative *concetto* to fill—and spatially define—an entire church. In the sanctuary, the crucified St. Andrew looks up (from a painting) to a frescoed God the Father in the lantern above the altar, from which natural light materializes into a *gloria* of gilded shafts and stucco angels. The metaphysical drama then breaks through the framing pediment as the apostle's white (stucco) soul ascends toward the dove of the Holy Spirit hovering in a second lantern above the congregation.

In Bernini's contemporaneous church at Ariccia—his Baroque revision of the Pantheon—his analogous *concetto* of Mary's Assumption integrates the dark sanctuary, her symbolic tomb, with the luminous dome of heaven as stucco angels hold out a crown along the Virgin's projected flight path from the background painting into the worshipers' own space. This device recalls Rubens's crowning invention, a generation earlier, for his *Assumption* at the high altar of Antwerp's cathedral, where he ensconced a statue of Christ on the pediment to extend a heavenly crown to his ascending mother in the painted altarpiece below.

On an urban plane, at the Ponte Sant'Angelo over the Tiber, Bernini translated Ignatius's *Spiritual Exercises* into a penitential prelude for pilgrims en route to Saint Peter's—a *Via Crucis* lined with ten angels carrying instruments of Christ's Passion. For his *Angel with Crown of Thorns* completed in 1669, he transformed a classical model, the so-called *Antinous* (actually a *Hermes*) in the Vatican gallery, into an emotional and attenuated, almost Neo-Gothic image—the keynote of his late style. The flamelike folds assume a life of their own, as if in response to the thorny crown. The eyes alone remain classically blank, so that ours may focus on that poignant object of meditation. Bernini here conflated in this sensual abstraction of pain the leitmotifs of St. Teresa's ecstatic suffering: cloud, angel, sharp instrument, transfigured face, and frozen cry, all underscored by reverberating drapery that Jacob Burckhardt described—and not as a compliment—as "carved with a spoon in almond jelly." Yet it was precisely through those fantastic folds that the seventy year-old sculptor sought to capture pure spirit in stone.

Bernini's late religious fervor transfigured even portraiture as he infused his conception of a "speaking likeness" with new meaning. For the papal physician Gabriele Fonseca's memorial chapel, dedicated to the Annunciation, he conjured up a vision—a chamber variation on his theme at Sant'Andrea. From the Holy Spirit in the lantern, a stucco descant evolves into full-bodied bronze angels elevating the altarpiece, a copy of Guido Reni's *Annunciation* in the Quirinal Palace.

The donor portrait, a work of the early 1670s, emerges from the side, as if from a triptych wing, and into our own space. Clutching a rosary, his other hand pressed to his breast, Gabriele Fonseca turns toward the altar: his profile parallels his namesake angel Gabriel's at the moment of Incarnation. This "praying likeness"—the distillation of Catholic piety—is the climactic resolution of a motif Bernini had introduced a half century earlier with the "speaking likeness" busts of Pope Gregory XV (1621, AGO, Toronto) and Monsignor Montoya (1622, Santa Maria di Monserrato, Rome).

There has been some scholarly speculation about the content of Fonseca's prayer. But here the iconographic context evokes the text as Fonseca recites the familiar refrain of his clutched rosary, which begins with the angel's first words of annunciation: "Hail, Mary, full of grace, the Lord is with thee." Its concluding supplication ("Holy Mary, Mother of God, pray for us sinners now and at the hour of our death") is miraculously fulfilled at the altar in a mystical communion between painting and sculpture. Birth transfigures death in this annunciation of eternal life.

Bernini explained that he often "put himself in the attitude he intended to give to the figure he was representing." In his first religious sculpture, the adolescent had replicated the fiery passion of his patron saint, Lawrence, by holding a burning torch to his own flesh as he sketched himself in a mirror. Gabriele Fonseca was no less intimately identified with his patron saint, but by a mystical (not physical) equation in the old maestro's calculus.

Bernini's *Blessed Ludovica Albertoni*, carved from 1672 to 1674, his final full-bodied marble, resolves in muted reverberations an ecstatic theme ranging from the early *Santa Bibiana* (1624–1626, Santa Bibiana, Rome) on through *Maria Raggi* (c. 1647, Santa Maria sopra Minerva, Rome) and *St. Teresa* (1647–1652, Santa Maria della Vittoria, Rome).

Ludovica lies on her deathbed and at the threshold of eternity. The walls of the small dark chapel converge like wings of a triptych opened to reveal Bernini's most luminous and painterly tableau. In extremis, with head thrown back, lips parted and half-closed eyes rolled up, Ludovica clutches her breast. Physical agony and metaphysical "movements of the soul" resonate through the cascading folds of her dress. White cherubs float like snowflakes down streams of light from concealed side windows, while Baciccio's background painting provides the window into Ludovica's interior vision of paradise.

Scholars have debated the precise moment represented: Is it her final consummation at death or her ecstatic transport of the preceding day? The question is moot. As in the *St. Teresa*, allusions to both physical death and mystical "dying" coalesce in a single image, a radiant conflation. A comparison with the *St. Teresa* illuminates Bernini's profound revisions over the quarter century. A tactile apparition has modulated into an ineffable transfiguration—from body into soul. Architectural isolation (Teresa's monumental tabernacle) has yielded to dramatic immanence.

Ludovica's jasper pall cascades toward the sarcophagus-altar (and the worshiper) like the overflowing stage in Bernini's play *The Flooding of the Tiber*. Diagonals are resolved in sustained horizontals. No family effigies are here introduced as eternal witnesses. The *Beata* Ludovica, the embodiment of a "blessed death," is contemplated by the viewer alone. *Requiem aeternam dona eis, Domine.* This is Bernini's *Requiem*.

For his last tomb commission, that of Alexander VII, Bernini injected a startling memento mori within a Christian apotheosis—the triumph of faith over death. From the apparent door of the pope's tomb (actually a side door of Saint Peter's), a gilded bronze skeleton flies upward brandishing an hourglass—not, ultimately, to terrify but, in every sense of the word, to uplift. *Mors ad caelos*: Death opens the way to heaven. Doubling as Father Time, with wings and an hourglass, this arresting agent of immortality begins to restore Alexander's clouded reputation as it raises the jasper shroud to uncover naked *Truth*—a recapitulation of Bernini's own vindication in marble, his unfinished *Truth Unveiled by Time* (1646–1652, Galleria Borghese, Rome).

The virtuous mountain of figures is capped by an immortal crown of stars, a monumental metamorphosis of Chigi's papal escutcheon of star-capped mountains that here incorporates the bareheaded pope himself as he kneels in eternal adoration of the sacrament. We have traveled a long way from Urban VIII's tomb, completed thirty years earlier, across the sanctuary. It is unblinking faith, not fortitude, that permeates Bernini's twilight masterpieces.

In the Sacrament Chapel of Saint Peter's, Bernini composed for the Holy Year 1675 his final altar work, a symbolic tomb for the sacramental body of Christ. For the last time he presided over a team of artisans—sculptors, founders, and goldsmiths—in a sublime summation of the central Christian mystery. His initial formulation of angels bearing both the architectural tabernacle and candles evolved through a series of preparatory drawings into a monumental duet of personified prayer.

Through his simplification and narrowing focus of imagery, the very hallmark of these last works, Bernini recasts the kneeling cherubim of the ancient Hebrew Ark in transfigured *contrapposto*. One extends his hands in prayer; the other withdraws, arms pressed to his breast—a gilded revision, da capo, of the marble angels Bernini had designed for the high altar of Sant'Agostino a half century earlier and later revived (in passing) in a preliminary design for his *Cathedra Petri* in the apse of Saint Peter's. Set before an altarpiece of the *Trinity*, the angelic pair evokes their source: Guido Reni's *Trinity* (Santissima Trinità dei Pellegrini, Rome), commissioned for the Holy Year 1625.

Vertically staged, Christ's sacrifice on Calvary (the crucifix) is superseded by the tabernacle, the symbolic locus of his burial and resurrection. Its architectural form refers both to the Early Christian *Anastasis* erected over the Holy Sepulcher in Jerusalem and to Bramante's *tempietto* nearby on the Gianicolo, at San Pietro in Montorio, the legendary Roman site of Saint Peter's martyrdom. As in the *Baldacchino*, Bernini here fused references to Christ and his first vicar in a sculptural hybrid. He had originally intended to crown his *Baldacchino* with a huge bronze statue of the Risen Christ but later had to replace it with a much lighter globe and cross. By reviving that triumphant figure for the tabernacle, Bernini finally resolved on a more intimate scale the *Baldacchino*'s suspended *concetto*: a three-staged narrative of death, resurrection, and enthronement that here culminates in Pietro da Cortona's heavenly altarpiece.

One evening at a convent in Paris, Bernini had complained that its massive silver tabernacle covered up two-thirds of a Guido Reni altarpiece. (One or the other had to be moved, he concluded.) Now, a decade later, he chose to exploit precisely such an "obstacle" by converting Pietro da Cortona's background canvas into an integral part of his composition and *concetto*. In this final reconciliation of painting and sculpture, Pietro's colorful angels frame the heavenly dome of Bernini's tabernacle (which eclipses Pietro's globe), while Bernini's sculpted angels are coordinated with the Holy Spirit to form a huge Trinitarian triangle as they beckon us to the sacred mystery they embrace.

In his first altar work at Saint Peter's, Bernini had cast architecture as colossal sculpture: a bronze baldachin raised over an altar, itself above a tomb. Here he retranslated sculpture into miniature architecture: a bronze tabernacle described as a tomb and raised above an altar.

In his last sculpture, an over-life-sized *Bust of the Savior* begun in 1679, the eighty-year-old maestro "summarized and condensed all his art," his son Domenico writes, adding that his father's "bold conception" more than compensated for the "weakness of his wrist." Bernini undertook this parting work not for his own tomb (a simple marble slab in Santa Maria Maggiore) but as a gift for Rome's preeminent convert, Queen Christina of Sweden, whose special prayers he requested on his deathbed since, he explained, she shared "a special language with God." It is precisely through Bernini's special language of gesture and facial expression alone that his otherworldly "speaking portrait" of the Lord communicates its meaning—the very means the sculptor had prearranged to use with his confessor, his nephew Father Filippo Marchese, in case (as in fact happened) in extremis he lost the power of speech.

The bust was to be mounted on a round Sicilian jasper base and supported by two angels kneeling on a gilded wooden socle. Bernini's sketch (1679, Museum der bildenden Künste, Leipzig) for the pedestal reflects his drawing (c. 1673, also in Leipzig) of similar angels elevating a monstrance to display the sacramental body of Christ. Bequeathed by Christina to Pope Innocent XI, Bernini's *Savior* was later adapted as the official emblem of the Apostolic Hospital in Rome before vanishing in the late eighteenth century.

Only a preliminary drawing preserved Bernini's redeeming image until Irving Lavin published in 1972 the marble in Norfolk, Virginia, as the lost bust. This was followed a year later by the discovery, in the cathedral of Sées, of the copy commissioned by Bernini's Parisian friend Pierre Cureau de la Chambre. While the latter bust reveals a classical beauty and polish typical of a competent copyist, the Norfolk version appears almost Gothic by comparison. It remained puzzling, even if accepted by most scholars.

The rediscovery, four decades later, of Bernini's lost original marble in the sacristy of San Sebastiano fuori le Mura in Rome—authenticated by Professor Lavin—confirms that the Norfolk bust represents an awkward copy (perhaps dating from the late eighteenth century); the bust at San Sebastiano, displayed in a grand niche near the entrance of the church, reveals in full glory Bernini's magnificent sunset in marble. It is well worth the pilgrimage along the Appian Way.

The unusual gesture that Lavin interpreted as an ambiguous combination of "abhorrence and protection" may recall the *Noli me tangere*: "Do not touch me, for I have not yet ascended to the Father" (John 20:17). Evoked through Christ's aloof visage and raised hand—an oblique benediction—this biblical allusion would have been reinforced by the angels that, with hands covered, lifted the divine effigy above the touch of mortals. When designing a symbolic globe to raise his *Louis XIV* in a royal apotheosis, he explained that its practical function was to prevent viewers from touching the bust.

But the surface meaning of the gesture was in fact described by Domenico (who surely knew what his father intended) as "the act of blessing." Thus the maestro of movement left as his parting tour de force not an iconic Christ with hand symbolically raised in a static, formal benediction but a dynamic divine figure caught at the moment when he is about to complete the horizontal sweep of the cruciform gesture, a moment familiar to every Catholic. In the end, as in the youthful *David*, it is all about *movement*. Viewed afresh, the *Savior* may finally come into focus as a sacramental apotheosis: a huge white host elevated as "the Bread of Angels," Bernini's sacrament in stone.

Bernini's career had commenced with a posthumous *Bust of Bishop Giovanni Battista Santoni*, a public effigy; seven decades later, it concluded with the private *Bust of the Savior*, animated through marble folds that follow no natural pattern. The striking realism of the child prodigy was in the end transfigured by this genius for whom life and art were as inseparable as fact and faith.

Chapter 13

Bernini's *Cristo Vivo*

In the dog days of August 1975, a month after starting my first job as an editorial assistant at Scribners, I decided to reward myself extravagantly for my modest paychecks: I bought the Bernini crucifix I had seen in a London gallery the previous summer, one of the series of bronzes Bernini had designed for Saint Peter's in Rome. I liquidated some savings and arranged to have it shipped to the office. It arrived in a crate that looked like a small coffin, much to the bemusement of my publishing colleagues.

I took the crucifix to Princeton and put it temporarily on loan in the Art Museum, where I gave some gallery talks on it. On Good Friday, the next year, I reclaimed it and carried it over to the chapel for the liturgy of the veneration of the cross. I liked the idea that Bernini's crucifix had returned to an altar—and a service of worship—before I took it home and later donated it to Princeton's museum.

Four decades later, I found myself wondering why Bernini designed in 1659 his sole *Cristo vivo* (living Christ) as both an addendum and the dramatic finale to the series of twenty-five crucifixes commissioned by Pope Alexander VII in 1658 for the side altars in Saint Peter's Basilica in Rome. The original design, a year earlier, had been a *Cristo morto* (dead Christ). Why did Bernini create this stunning revision so late in the game?

Bernini, *Cristo vivo* (1659, Art Museum, Princeton University)

At the time of this commission, Bernini was immersed in far grander projects for the Chigi pope, who was to leave an architectural imprint on the Eternal City surpassing even his Barberini predecessor, Urban VIII, in magnitude. Born into a family of rich Sienese bankers, Fabio Chigi was a close friend of Bernini's and, like Pope Urban, aimed to exploit his papal patronage—and purse—*ad astra.*

On the first day of his papacy in 1655, Alexander VII summoned Bernini (who was already at work on the Chigi family burial chapel in Santa Maria del Popolo) and encouraged him to carry out the vast plans he had conceived for "the greater embellishment of God's temple, the glorification of the papacy, and the decoration of Rome." He named Bernini his private architect as well as architect of Saint Peter's, a post he had held since 1629, and gave Bernini full rein to transform Rome into Europe's Baroque capital.

In 1656, Bernini was commissioned to undertake his grandest project of all, the all-embracing arms of the colonnade (1656–1667) at the entrance court of Saint Peter's. The design was the urban embodiment of his creed of architectural humanism: "The beauty of everything in the world, as well as in architecture," Bernini explained during the colonnade's construction, "consists in proportion. One might say that is the divine element since it originates in the body of Adam which has been created by God's hands and in His own image." This is why, he maintained, sculptors made the best architects. The next year, the pope commissioned Bernini to complete the basilica with an explosive finale in the apse: the *Cathedra Petri* and *Gloria* (1657–1666), his *Gesamtkunstwerk* of bronze, stucco, gilding, stained glass, and light.

Among the assistants with whom Bernini chose to collaborate on the larger-than-life bronze sculptures of the Fathers of the Church was Ercole Ferrata. A year later, in 1658, he chose Ferrata to assist on his next commission—the crucifixes. Although small in scale, this commission was vast in scope: in addition to the twenty-five bronze crosses—each bearing a separately cast corpus—there were 150 bronze candlesticks (six per altar) also designed by Bernini, an unprecedented series of bronze furnishings for a church. Ferrata was later to carve for Bernini's series of angels on the Ponte Sant'Angelo—most fittingly—the monumental *Angel with Cross* (1668–1669). But his earlier assignment, in miniature, was no less crucial.

Born in 1610 in Pellio Inferiore near Como, Ferrata came to Rome and in 1647 was numbered among Bernini's army of over forty assistants who worked on the nave decorations for Saint Peter's. He then moved on to complete his sculptural training under Bernini's classicizing rival Alessandro Algardi, for whom he remained a chief assistant until the master's death. Algardi's papal patron—and Bernini's former nemesis—Innocent X died the following year, which marked Bernini's re-ascendancy as undisputed artistic dictator. For most sculptors, working in Rome meant working for Bernini. Ferrata had a new boss.

Bernini evidently planned all the crosses to bear a corpus of the *Cristo morto*, as that is the only model the master designed to be executed by Ferrata and cast in 1658. Of the twenty-three extant crucifixes on the side altars of Saint Peter's, eighteen represent that *Cristo morto* model; only five represent the *Cristo vivo* that Bernini designed a year later, in 1659. While the former recalled his bronze crucifix of 1654 for Philip IV of Spain—to which we shall turn presently—the latter revived the impassioned visage and animated S-curve of Bernini's recently completed sculpture of the praying *Daniel* for the Chigi Chapel (1657). That figure's dynamic *contrapposto* ultimately harks back to Bernini's youthful study of the *Laocoön* in the Vatican. Beyond these stylistic affinities, the deeper links between this second crucifix type and the *Daniel* shed light on both the genesis of Bernini's *Cristo vivo* and its meaning.

The first of Bernini's extant crucifixes is the large bronze *Cristo morto* commissioned around 1654 for Philip IV of Spain for the royal burial chapel in the Escorial. Bernini's son and biographer Domenico described it as "larger than life size," although it was four and a half feet tall. (Such is the power of illusion.) The chapel was completed in 1654; Bernini's honorarium, according to Domenico, was "a large gold chain."

After the death of Pope Innocent X in 1655, Cardinal Antonio Barberini ordered a crucifix from Bernini for his house in Paris; that crucifix was donated to Louis XIV of France following the cardinal's death. It was listed in the royal inventory of 1684 but disappeared a century later.

Still another crucifix is mentioned by Bernini's biographer Filippo Baldinucci as having been "made for himself" and, during the sculptor's visit to Paris in 1665, given to the Jesuit cardinal Sforza Pallavicino, who was looking after Bernini's family back in Rome and mentoring his son Monsignor Pietro Filippo Bernini. A bronze corpus in the Art Gallery of Ontario has been misidentified as that third (Pallavicino) crucifix, but in my view it clearly represents a later pastiche. It is "Bernini based"—but not Bernini's own vision, much less a revision overseen by the maestro himself.

Bernini had the (lost) terra-cotta *modello* for the Escorial corpus cast for a devotional crucifix for Pope Alexander VII. Now in a private collection in Germany, it reveals the maestro's touch. Equally striking is its omission of a crown of thorns, consistently absent in all the crucifixes Bernini designed at this time for Saint Peter's, as well as in the marble crucifix held by his sculpture of *Saint Jerome* (1661–1663) in the Chigi Chapel of Siena's cathedral.

In view of his original commission for a *Cristo morto*, what are we to make of Bernini's intervention and creation of a second corpus for the altars of Saint Peter's a year after most of the castings were completed? The very fact that at least three-quarters of them (eighteen of the extant twenty-three) represent the *Cristo morto* raises an obvious—if heretofore unasked—question: Why at this late stage did Bernini return to the drawing board and design the *Cristo vivo*? What prompted that fundamental revision of style and iconography?

Bernini's revision, his *Cristo vivo*, harks back to Guido Reni's high altarpiece (ca. 1640) in San Lorenzo in Lucina—where Bernini was later to contribute the Fonseca Chapel (1668–1675)—as it also calls to mind his deceased rival Algardi's *Cristo vivo* modeled around 1646 for Pope Innocent X. In the spirit of the *paragone* (competition) between painting and sculpture—and perhaps also a professional rivalry beyond the grave—Bernini's *Cristo vivo* reveals how much he revised Algardi's conception by introducing the dynamic torsion of the suffering figure in extremis. Bernini heightened this emphasis by rejecting the flying drapery of both Reni and Algardi in favor of a tightly wound, compact, and yet dynamic loincloth that no longer distracts from the corpus as the focal point—his bronze evocation of Christ's prayers from the cross: "My God, my God, why have you forsaken me?" (Matt. 27:46) and "Father, into your hands I commend my spirit" (Luke 23:46). Algardi's Savior conveyed submissive acceptance; Bernini's expresses ecstatic communion.

The key to the meaning of Bernini's most passionate *imago Christi* is its link to his contemporaneous portrayal of *Daniel*, a connection that is deeper than the stylistic genesis of the figure's animated S-curve. The Old Testament prophet Daniel's salvation in the lions' den was a traditional prefiguration of Christ's resurrection, his ultimate triumph over death. This iconographic concordance would have had special resonance with the Chigi pope—it may even have been his idea—since Alexander VII owned the sole manuscript of the *Book of Bel and the Dragon*, the biblical source of the scene that charges the space across the diagonal axis of the Chigi Chapel in Santa Maria del Popolo as the angel points out the praying Daniel to Habakkuk, who is carrying a basket of loaves to the imprisoned prophet.

It is this Eucharistic subtext that Bernini translated into his Christological variation on the theme at Saint Peter's: his *Cristo vivo* conflates Christ's sacrificial death on the cross with a projected image of resurrection, as a sculptural gloss on the sacramental miracle renewed at each celebration of the Mass at the altars. Through the bloodless reenactment of Christ's sacrifice on Calvary, bread and wine are transubstantiated, according to Catholic doctrine, into the body and blood of the living Christ, the Eucharistic *Cristo vivo*. Bernini's inspired revision of the corpus thereby effects a conflation of two distinct moments of the Gospels and Creed: the Savior's imminent death and, proleptically, his resurrection. Bernini conjoined the sacrificial with the sacramental in this iconic Baroque embodiment of Eucharistic triumph, the ultimate expression of thanksgiving—the meaning of the Greek word *eucharistia*. Thus did he conclude his sequence of twenty-five altar crucifixes for Saint Peter's not in B-minor but B-major.

The sheer quality of the Princeton corpus mounted on a wooden cross with burled walnut veneer and inserted into a Bernini-worthy base (reminiscent of his early design for the tomb of Cardinal Pimentel) suggests that this casting was intended for a special patron. The base is hollow, with a wooden tabernacle door on the back, indicating its probable use on a private altar. Perhaps it was made for a member of the Chigi family or as a papal gift to a high-ranking prelate.

There are two other examples of this corpus (neither is mounted on a cross): one in the Staatliche Museen in Berlin, the other in the Martinelli Collection in Perugia. Whether either represents a missing corpus from Saint Peter's remains a matter of conjecture. In any case, the Princeton corpus presents a rare additional example of a casting that reveals Bernini's masterly supervision.

The lesson of Bernini's *Cristo vivo* was not lost on Ferrata. The year after its design, 1660, Ferrata carved his most Berninesque sculpture to date, *Saint Agnes on a Pyre*, for the church of Sant'Agnese in Agone on Rome's Piazza Navona. He went on to become the preeminent teacher of sculptors in Baroque Rome. Among the molds inventoried in his estate was that of the *Cristo vivo*.

Chapter 14

The Garden of Love

From Rubens to Mozart

In the last decade of his life, Rubens painted one of his noblest (and most personal) celebrations of life and love, *The Garden of Love*, which hangs in Madrid's Prado, the brightest star in that galaxy of Rubens paintings.

Rubens, *The Garden of Love* (1632, Prado, Madrid)

It is one of those masterpieces that may be appreciated on its own terms, a work that speaks for itself. Unlike Rubens's altarpieces, historical epics, or classical mythologies, it requires no learned interpretation. Just as in Mozart's *The Marriage of Figaro* we need not understand the Italian libretto in order to experience the emotions translated into the language of music, so it is in Rubens's sublime painting. These figural variations on a theme—the theme being the cultivation of love—are played out in harmony with the idyllic landscape, the architectural cadences, the sculptural counterpoints, and even the hovering putti, those airborne cherubs and cupids, the painter's version of grace notes. And yet probably no single painting by Rubens has evoked so many conflicting scholarly explanations: I am reminded of Shakespeare's sonnets and the shelves of scholarship—and sometimes fantasy—they have inspired. We seem to be on firmer ground in Rubens's religious and mythological scenes. Poetic fantasias about love tend to invite a scholars' free-for-all. What is this painting about? Whom is it about?

The range of interpretations has run from the autobiographical to the arcane, from slice-of-life genre painting to complex allegory. To some, the picture illustrates a garden party around Rubens and his recent bride, Helena Fourment, complete with in-laws. To others, it represents a Neoplatonic allegory of love personified by the three seated ladies—sensual, celestial, and earthly love: a cinematic progression through love's initiation, maturation, and culmination in matrimony. Is the figure at the left really the elderly Rubens rejuvenated by love with his wife Helena, as one scholar has suggested? Or is Helena to be found seated in the middle—or standing at the right? Do the three seated ladies, without escorts, represent three allegorical stages of love—or perhaps the Three Graces, fleshly counterparts to their statue in the grotto behind them? Or are they personifications of sight, hearing, and touch?

Sifting through the reams of scholarship on the subject, I felt I had stumbled on the ultimate multiple-choice College Board question: A, B, C, all of the above, none of the above? One novel interpretation was based on the painting's earliest recorded Flemish title, *Conversatie à la Mode* (a social gathering, in vogue), as a work extolling social gallantry, fashion, and aristocratic courtship mirrored in the English cavalier poetry and French "how-to" manuals of the day. My brief survey will not permit excursions through such Baroque mazes. Instead, we must return to the evidence within the painting itself, as seen against the background of the artist's life and works and the broader artistic landscape in which this *Garden of Love* was planted.

First of all, Rubens painted his *Garden of Love* within two or three years of his marriage to Helena in 1630. She was a girl of sixteen; he, a widower of fifty-three. Describing his reasons for the marriage in a letter to a friend, Rubens wrote, "I made up my mind to marry again, since I was not yet inclined to live the abstinent life of the celibate, thinking that if we must give the first place to continence, we may enjoy licit pleasures with thankfulness. I have taken a young wife of honest but middle-class family, although everyone tried to persuade me to make a court marriage. But I feared Pride, that inherent vice of the nobility, particularly in that sex, and that is why I chose one who would not blush to see me take my brushes in hand."

It was a blissful and fruitful marriage, to say the least: Their fifth child was born eight months after Rubens's death in 1640. During that twilight decade, Rubens painted a number of portraits of Helena, such as the famous *Het Pelsken* (the fur) in Vienna, in which she is portrayed as the classical *Venus Pudica*—"in the flesh," so to speak. Among the family portraits, his *Walk in the Garden* (1631, Alte Pinakothek, Munich) describes a garden of love, but there an actual and thoroughly domesticated one, the artist's own. Rubens walks arm in arm with Helena toward the sculpture pavilion, his son Nicolaas a few steps behind. In the background stands a cupid-and-dolphin fountain (symbolizing love's swiftness); in the foreground, the dog and peacocks (emblems of fidelity and marriage) underscore the theme of conjugal harmony. The Munich panel foreshadows Rubens's late self-portrait with Helena and their youngest son, Peter Paul, also set in a garden, now preserved in the Metropolitan Museum, New York.

So much for the happy home front, the spirit of which permeates its imaginary, allegorized reflection in the Prado—"imaginary" because Rubens's *Garden of Love* is not lifted from the artist's family album. Rather, it is derived from a formal tradition of love gardens, which he infused with personal feeling and significance.

During the 1630s, Rubens retired from his diplomatic career and devoted more time than ever to painting for his own pleasure—landscapes, portraits, genre subjects. In his *Kermesse* in the Louvre, Rubens offered his version of a Pieter Bruegel, of the Flemish pictorial tradition of peasants at play. At the other end of the scale, but related in its accelerating rhythms, is his *Feast of Venus* (1636, Kunsthistorisches Museum, Vienna), a full-bodied Baroque revival of a classical bacchanal. Somewhere in between we find the *Dance of Peasants*—Italian peasants this time—in the Prado and *Couples Playing near a Castle* (1635, Kunsthistorisches Museum, Vienna), recalling Rubens's Castle of Steen, his country retreat where he spent his final years as Lord of Steen. The couples are now Flemish, well-to-do, *haut bourgeois*, and more tempered—but hardly restrained—in their amorous pursuits. We begin to approach the garden.

The tradition of love gardens goes back to medieval art, in which it was often associated with matrimony, as we find in the illuminated month of April in the *Très Riches Heures du Duc de Berry* by the Limbourg Brothers, illustrating a betrothal in a castle garden. Sometimes the theme was treated satirically, as in an anonymous Flemish *Geuchmatt* (fool's meadow), in which erstwhile fickle men have their wings clipped and their ankles ensnared, their spouses holding them on very short leashes. A Flemish *Love Garden* of around 1600, attributed to Louis de Caullery, provides a more immediate precedent for Rubens's treatment, with corresponding musician, walled garden, couples strolling and dallying, a dog (faithfulness), and peacocks (sacred to Juno, symbolizing marriage), but notably without any mythological sculpture or invasive putti. This is a conventional *Conversatie à la Mode*.

What transforms Rubens's version into something more resonant, into a metaphorical garden of love, are the sculptural additions, like so many iconographic footnotes, as well as the flying putti bearing emblems of love. Rubens's invented sculpture always conveys a specific meaning—here it is the goddess Venus presiding over her realm. She is literally expressive, her breasts functioning as fountains, recalling Rubens's fertile fountain of "Mother Earth" (Gaia), the mother of Erichthonius, in his earlier *Discovery of Erichthonius* in the Liechtenstein Collection. We are reminded that Venus—like Rubens's Venus/Helena of *Het Pelsken*—is also a mother: her son, Cupid, the god of love, prompts the couple entering at the left.

In the pavilion, hidden water jets surprise the cavorting couples. This popular sixteenth-century Italian garden amusement is more clearly seen in the woodcut by Christoffel Jegher, based on Rubens's drawing in the Metropolitan Museum. The rusticated facade is derived from Rubens's own architectural contributions to his Antwerp house and garden. A Renaissance man, Rubens practiced architecture as well as invented sculpture. Within the pavilion a sculpture of the Three Graces denotes the prevailing civility of this highly cultured garden. But, above all, the flying cupids provide the key to the nature of the love here celebrated, for the flaming torch, the turtledoves, the floral crown, and the yoke are all marriage symbols.

This is not "free love" but conjugal love fostered by Venus and her minions. Thus the picture celebrates Rubens's own recent marriage, here reflected by analogy and allegory rather than specified by portraiture. Rubens has thoroughly transformed the pictorial tradition of the garden of love, recasting it in his High Baroque style, infusing it with psychological depth, and raising it to a new poetic plane. Among seventeenth-century love gardens it stands apart, unrivaled in its appeal. For its true artistic descendants, we must look to the next century, to the *fêtes galantes* of Antoine Watteau.

A Fleming by birth (from Valenciennes, formerly part of Flanders), Watteau appeared in Paris just as the long, drawn-out battle in the French Academy between the *Poussinistes* and *Rubénistes*—the classicizing defenders of line versus the Baroque proponents of color—was turning in Rubens's favor. One of Watteau's early masters, the decorative painter Claude Audran, was also the curator (*concierge*) of the Luxembourg Palace; he had the key to the gallery of Rubens's celebrated Medici Cycle, and the hours Watteau spent studying and sketching these monumental Flemish Baroque canvases were to transform the future of French Rococo painting.

Watteau's translation of his Flemish heritage into a Parisian idiom is typified by his drawing of a dancing peasant couple from Rubens's *Kermesse* and their transference to a more rarefied setting in Watteau's *La Surprise* (1718, Getty Museum, Los Angeles). The banded columns of Watteau's *Music Party* (1718, Wallace Collection, London) have their architectural roots in Rubens's *Garden of Love*. But his true debt to Rubens is far less specific and far more pervasive. Watteau's *fêtes galantes* (virtually untranslatable: something between "gallant festivals" and "merry parties"), a new genre and category devised especially for him by the French Academy, owe to Rubens's *Garden of Love* not only their subject matter and *Rubéniste* stylistic values but also the repeated inclusion of invented statues of Venus to sound the appropriate keynotes.

Their pitch and tone are distinctly mellower than in Rubens. Watteau strikes a melancholy note within the gaiety. His lovers are tentative where Rubens's were exuberant. His sculptured Venus is often languid, as in *Fêtes Vénitiennes* (1719, National Gallery of Scotland, Edinburgh), sometimes even asleep, where Rubens's was demonstrative and assertive. In his *Champs Elysées* (1718, Wallace Collection, London), Watteau translates into stone his flesh-and-blood sleeping Antiope, painted three years earlier (*Jupiter and Antiope*, Louvre, Paris), which in turn is a quotation from a Hellenistic bronze of *Sleeping Cupid* (Metropolitan Museum, New York)—an artistic metamorphosis from sculpture, through flesh, back to sculpture.

Watteau's statues seem indeed to hover on the boundary of stone and flesh, of art and life, of what is real and what is imagined, like the statue of Hermione stepping down from her pedestal at the end of Shakespeare's *The Winter's Tale*. So, too, Watteau's lovers seem at times to hover between theater and life, between the play and—to quote the Tom Stoppard title—*The Real Thing*. In his *Mezzetin* (1718–1720, Metropolitan Museum, New York), Watteau presents an actor from the Commedia dell'arte plaintively serenading his inamorata. We can almost hear Don Giovanni's "Deh, vieni alla finestra" (come to the window). She—off stage, off canvas—remains unseen, but her response may be inferred in the cold shoulder of the female statue turning its back on poor Mezzetin: Despite his good voice, this stock character was ever hapless in love.

A melancholy strain runs throughout the lightness and gaiety of Watteau's *fêtes galantes* like the poignant counterthemes woven through some of Mozart's brightest movements: a sense of the ephemeral, of the transitory nature of these visions of love and happiness. The yearning for permanence within the garden of love is tempered by the realization that, like Watteau's perfectly poised dancer in *L'Indifferent* (1717, Louvre, Paris), the magical equilibrium is but momentary. Mozart evokes it in music; T. S. Eliot, in one of his *Four Quartets*:

At the still point of the turning world. Neither flesh
nor fleshless;
Neither from nor towards; At the still point, there the dance is,
But neither arrest nor movement. And do not call it fixity,
Where past and future are gathered. Neither movement from
nor towards,
Neither ascent nor decline. Except for the point, the still point,
There would be no dance, and there is only the dance.

This theme is fully played out in Watteau's consummate garden of love—we might say his sacred grove of love—the so-called *Pilgrimage to Cythera* (Louvre, Paris), the official painting submitted for his admission into the French Academy in 1717. I say "so-called" because, despite some muddying of the scholarly waters, it is now generally accepted that Watteau chose to depict the lovers about to depart *from* Cythera, Venus's sacred island, the ultimate goal of these amorous pilgrims, complete with festive pilgrims' staffs.

The statue of Venus, an antique "term" marking the boundary of her realm, has been adorned with roses; at its base hang a bow and a quiver full of arrows, the weapons of love. Golden rays of twilight suffuse the background as the lovers, their quest fulfilled, proceed to reboard the vessel to return home to the mainland. Watteau's unusual choice of subject—his poignant sense of timing—is underscored by comparison with his earlier, overtly theatrical version of *L'Isle de Cythère* (1709–1710, Städel, Frankfurt), representing an outdoor performance of a play, and with a contemporary print by Claude Duflos. Both leave no doubt that in his academy piece Watteau chose to depict the departure, not the setting out. The couples are clearly already on Cythera, not in some harbor waiting for the ferry. A popular

Watteau, *Departure from the Isle of Cythera* (1717, Louvre, Paris)

novel at the time was titled *The Return from the Isle of Love*; the theme was clearly in the air.

Lest there be any doubt, Watteau's second version, in Berlin (1717–1719, Charlottenburg Castle), introduces several telling details: the foreground couple already fulfilled in love; the gathering of flowers ("to flirt" derives from the Old French *fleureter*, "to talk flowers"); Cupid about to shoot a lover with an arrow reversed, feathers first, to cancel love; and the animated statue of Venus. She is here shown withholding the quiver from her son: The time for love is past. At the base of the statue lie trophies of military armor and the arts (music, literature) as offerings placed before the goddess of love: *Omnia vincit amor*—love conquers all. Rubens's *Garden of Love* expressed a gathering crescendo; Watteau's, a graceful diminuendo. Rubens's lovers approached conjugal fulfillment; Watteau's already begin to withdraw from transitory bliss.

Rubens spent the last decade of his long, productive career rejuvenated by marriage. Watteau remained a bachelor, always something of an outsider despite his fame, his promising career cut short by tuberculosis. Yet, almost singlehandedly, he created a new, typically French Rococo tradition of the love garden. Tended by Watteau's followers Jean-Baptiste Pater and Nicolas Lancret, it was to achieve its final flowering in the art of Jean-Honoré Fragonard.

Now Fragonard was not the first to introduce the "swinging lady" into love's gardens; she had already made a cameo appearance in Watteau's *The Shepherds* (c. 1717, Charlottenburg Castle, Berlin). Yet Fragonard swept her to unprecedented heights. In what is surely the world's most famous *Swing* (1767, Wallace Collection, London), she is propelled higher and higher by, some say, a bishop—others, her unsuspecting husband or elderly suitor—until her secret lover gains the optimum view of her legs (and perhaps more). He lies sprawled in a bed of roses (a visual pun) as she flings off her shoe, a popular eighteenth-century motif symbolizing the casting off of virtue. The sculpture of *Cupid* by Étienne-Maurice Falconet admonishes silence, while, in the background, two putti riding a dolphin symbolize the swift surge of love's pleasures. These sculptural glosses clearly maintain their iconographic function as established by Rubens and followed by Watteau.

For Fragonard as well, they play more than a decorative role, as we see in his consummate masterpiece at the Frick Collection in New York: *The Progress of Love*. A garden of love in four acts, the series was commissioned by King Louis XV's last mistress, Madame du Barry, who ultimately lost her head on the guillotine over royal love, for her country pavilion at Louveciennes. Fragonard painted the four large canvases between 1771 and 1773: They represent his most important commission and grandiose cycle of paintings. But already at their completion they had outlived their time. Neoclassicism *à la grecque* was on the horizon. The more austere style of Joseph-Marie Vien coming into vogue would, quite literally, displace Fragonard. After only a few weeks on view, Fragonard's masterpieces were returned to the artist, who took them back home to Grasse. There installed in his cousin's house, the series was supplemented by ten additional canvases. The paintings crossed the Atlantic in 1915 and settled at the Frick, where they create the most perfect French eighteenth-century room—and "garden"—in the New World.

It has been claimed—in the Frick's own catalog—that Fragonard's prominent statues have only the most generalized anecdotal connection with his foreground subject. This I cannot accept. In my view, they provide precise and witty iconographic commentaries on the meaning of each scene, symbolic touchstones of love's progress. In the opening *Surprise*, the aspiring lover has scaled the wall of the garden of love, startling the alarmed young lady who has been reading a letter—we may guess whose: Its seal, like the gentleman's jacket, is red. Between and behind them, we find the familiar statue of Venus withholding the quiver from Cupid. We may recall that same statue in Watteau's second *Departure from the Isle of Cythera* and, with closer application to the present scene, in his *Garden Party* in Dresden: The time for love's fulfillment, it signifies, has not yet come. The green pitcher on the ground is as yet unbroken, an emblematic footnote to our heroine's virtue, which likewise remains intact.

We proceed to *The Pursuit*, where the tempo, allegro con brio, is marked by the sculpture of cupids riding a dolphin, recalling those in Fragonard's *Swing* and the familiar fountain motif in Rubens's mythologies. The maiden's precarious footing, as she flees, suggests an imminent fall—in love, *tomber amoureux*.

The next scene used to be called *Love Letters* but, based on Willibald Sauerländer's identification of the allegorical statue of *Amicitia*, is better titled *Love and Friendship*. The pair are now shown reading together—at least she's reading—with the dog of faithfulness at their feet. The letters bear the familiar red seal. The merging cloud-like foliage above seems to embrace, mirroring the figures below. It has been proposed that this subject should come last, illustrating Madame de Pompadour's maxim that "love passes but friendship endures." A touching thought. But it is hard to reconcile such sentiments with either Fragonard or the new royal mistress, Madame du Barry, who, unlike her predecessor, the aging La Pompadour, had no physical infirmity requiring her to fall back on such a consoling philosophy.

Finally, in *The Lover Crowned*, the traditional symbols of the love garden (music, garlands, floral crown) appear along with the

Fragonard, *The Lover Crowned* (1771–1773, Frick Collection, New York)

artist himself sketching this happy conclusion. Once again, the soft foliage and counterpointed, calligraphic branch reflect the lovers below. And what of little Cupid? He is now asleep: His job done, he has earned his nap.

If nature plays a supporting dramatic role in this cycle, in the late Fragonard it dominates. The figures recede in importance, enveloped by sensuous and overblown foliage foreshadowing the landscape fantasies of Hubert Robert and early Romanticism. For example, in Fragonard's *Swing* (c. 1775–1780, National Gallery, Washington) or *Fête at Rambouillet* (c. 1780, Gulbenkian Foundation, Oeiras), a Watteau minuet has been reorchestrated as a symphony. The trees themselves now seem to embody the pent-up forces of nature, like gathering storm clouds about to break at any moment.

Fragonard outlived the Rococo. He survived the French Revolution, but his style did not. For the finale of the garden of love, we must look to another medium, to the last act of Mozart's *The Marriage of Figaro*: If only Fragonard had designed the backdrops! (Jean-Pierre Ponnelle's 1985 sets for the Metropolitan Opera suggested, by contrast, a "petrified garden" derived from Piranesi engravings, overshadowed by gray crumbling architecture.) Someone at London Records, at least, sensed the natural affinity with Fragonard, choosing the artist's bilevel *capriccio* in his *Gardens of the Villa d'Este* (Wallace Collection, London) at Tivoli to illustrate Sir Georg Solti's magnificent 1982 recording of this opera about "upstairs/downstairs" in the garden of love—with Frederica von Stade as the definitive Cherubino.

In Mozart's fourth and final act, the garden becomes the scene of amorous pursuits, disguised rendezvous, intrigues, infidelities, and entrapment. Then, through the perfect fusion of Mozart's music and Da Ponte's libretto, it is transformed into a place of grace and redemption, as the Countess suddenly reveals her true identity to the wayward Count, who has just finished accusing her of unfaithfulness. Caught in his infidelity and now chagrined, he begs for her pardon. "I am kinder and say yes" (*Più docil' io sono, e dico di sì*), replies the forgiving Countess in the most heavenly absolution ever pronounced through music.

It has been said that the ultimate goal of art is to reconcile us to life. If so, then nowhere is that reconciliation more inviting or more assured than in the ever-refreshing gardens of love by Rubens, Watteau, and Fragonard. In these worldly, secular, and sensual settings, we are offered glimpses into Eden redeemed, heaven on earth, where divine and erotic love—*agápe* and *eros*—are revealed to be but two reflections of the same face.

The Vocal Arts

Chapter 15

Sacred Music

"The Holy Art"

Our first appreciation of God, as we gaze up to the heavens, is as an artist. Whatever else the universe may hold, its created shape and reflected glory suggest a vast canvas comprising a multitude of masterpieces. The theme of Creation has given rise to some of the greatest achievements by human creators in the realm of art. Arguably the most famous sacred artwork in Christendom is Michelangelo's great Sistine ceiling, known to students and tourists alike long before they see it in the flesh. In his celebrated BBC series *Civilisation*, Kenneth Clark claimed, "It is possible to interpret the whole of the Sistine ceiling as a poem on the subject of creation."

But Michelangelo was not alone in recomposing Creation. Almost three centuries later, he was answered in the thunderous chords, evocative harmonies, and soaring lines of an oratorio: *The Creation* by Franz Joseph Haydn. Composed by the prolific maestro well into his sixties, it represents Haydn's response to Handel's *Messiah*, which so overwhelmed Haydn on his first hearing it in 1791 at Westminster Abbey that he wept during the "Hallelujah Chorus." "He is the master of us all," was Haydn's verdict.

Six years later, he began to compose his own sacred masterpiece of comparable scope and power. A prequel of sorts to *Messiah*,

Haydn's *Creation* sets to music an assemblage of texts derived, by an unknown librettist, from Milton's *Paradise Lost*. Then, in Vienna, the great patron of Baroque music Baron Gottfried van Swieten, who had earlier introduced Mozart to the music of Bach and Handel, provided a German translation for Haydn to set the greatest music he would ever write. In his own words to his biographer, "I was never so religious as during the composition of *The Creation*. Daily I fell on my knees and asked God for strength."

The oratorio was hugely successful from the first hearing and was repeated countless times throughout Europe. Haydn's last public appearance shortly before he died was at a performance in 1808 in Vienna; his former pupil Ludwig van Beethoven was among the listeners. At the climactic moment of Creation—the thunderous, exalting fortissimo of chords that accompany and overwhelm the words of God's command "And let there be light"—Haydn was himself so deeply moved that he confessed, "It was not I, but a Power above who created that."

Ever since I was a schoolboy soprano, my favorite chorus in all music was Haydn's triumphal setting of the opening of Psalm 19, the climax of part one of his *Creation*: "The heavens are telling the glory of God, The wonder of his work proclaims the firmament." Six decades later, this music still conveys, as no words can, the Creator behind Creation, just as Handel's soprano solo in *Messiah*—"I know that my redeemer liveth"—redeems the suffering of Job as well as our own and points forward, as an aural prefiguration, to Christ as Redeemer, our Messiah.

The greatest music of the eighteenth century was religious. Antonio Vivaldi, whose output and virtuosity rival Bernini in sound, was ordained a priest; his dispensation to retire early from celebrating masses was sacred music's gain. Ludwig Gerber wrote in his 1792 *Lexicon* of composers that Vivaldi "always had his rosary in his hands and laid it down only when it came time to compose." Johann Sebastian Bach composed masterpieces that represent the musical equivalent of the Sistine ceiling. His study of Palestrina's Masses provided a grounding in that Roman tradition. Bach's monumental biblical oratorios, the *St. Matthew Passion* and the *St. John Passion*, rival the most profound altarpieces of all time. As Richard Strauss's Composer (*Komponist*) in *Ariadne auf Naxos* proclaims, "Musik ist eine heilige Kunst"—Music is a holy art.

In addition to so many cantatas—sung to perfection by Elisabeth Schwarzkopf in her early recordings—the Lutheran Bach composed the magisterial *Mass in B Minor*; it has no peer. Compared with that seasonal favorite, Handel's *Messiah*, Bach's *Christmas Oratorio* is more ecclesiastical than operatic; it glows with the flickering of church candles, not the blaze of chandeliers. There is a magic in Bach that never wanes; it sounds more miraculous at each hearing. He is the master of all sacred music.

But Bach was not without worthy successors. The masses of Haydn and Mozart rank high in the heavens of sacred sound. The devout Haydn has never been underestimated in this realm. His *Seven Last Words of Christ*—originally composed as instrumental counterparts to the biblical readings on Good Friday and then later reworked as a choral piece—may indeed offer the last word on this theme. But Wolfgang Amadeus Mozart was not so fortunate. What bad luck, illness, and a tragically untimely death (at the age of thirty-five) did not do, modern authors have wrought with a vengeance. Will future generations be able to picture this genius as any other than the crude caricature in Peter Shaffer's play and film *Amadeus*: a drunken imbecile with God-given talent and a dippy wife?

The common wisdom used to be that Mozart's religious music was merely "for hire," something he knocked off to earn a living so that he could write the music—operas, symphonies, chamber pieces—he really loved. What a surprise, then, to read that his widow, Constanze, said that his favorite genre of all was church music. A close study of Mozart's sacred music confirms Constanze's claim. His *Vesperae solennes de confessore*, with its twilight "Laudate Dominum," a sunset in sound, was as carefully composed as anything Mozart ever wrote, and it reveals that he paid close attention to the texts of the psalms and canticles that make up the chanted sequences of these vespers.

Mozart's glorious *Coronation Mass* in C-major offers a telling footnote, a glimpse into the composer's creative process. The soprano's hauntingly beautiful *Agnus Dei* prefigures its later reworking and recapitulation for the Countess's poignant aria in act three of *The Marriage of Figaro*: "Dove sono i bei momenti?"—Where have all the sweet moments gone? So much for the myth that Mozart recycled bits of opera when composing his church music; here it was precisely the opposite. Both arias begin sorrowfully (as befits the "Lamb of God, who taketh away the sins of the world") and then are suddenly transformed into an upbeat conclusion. For Mozart, the peace of *Dona nobis pacem* is not a passive one—not the absence of pain or conflict, but rather the consummation of joy.

In the nineteenth century, the Romantic century, artists took to the garrets and painted less for church or court and instead primarily for private collectors—and for themselves. Their doctrine of "art for art's sake" took root and replaced the old idea of art as the means of conveying religious truths. (How many Rodins or Monets are to be found in churches?) But the tradition continued to flourish in music—through Beethoven's *Missa Solemnis*, Mendelssohn's Protestant oratorios, Schubert's richly melodic Masses, Berlioz's *Te Deum* and *Requiem*, down to Fauré's ethereal *Requiem* and the triumphant *Te Deum* of the late Romantic (and equally devout) Anton Bruckner at the close of the century.

Even the anticlerical Giuseppe Verdi was not immune. His *Requiem*, performed and recorded in modern times perhaps more than any other composer's, has rightly been proclaimed his greatest opera. Its "Dies Irae" captures in sound the *terribilità* of Michelangelo's *Last Judgment* more faithfully and powerfully than anything before or after—in any medium.

In May 1873, the great Italian novelist Alessandro Manzoni, author of *The Betrothed*, died. Verdi considered him not only "one of the finest [novelists] of all ages" but also "a comfort to humanity." As a heartfelt memorial to his literary hero and friend, Verdi completed the *Requiem*, adding all the liturgical movements that lead up to his concluding *Libera Me*. Performed on the first anniversary of Manzoni's death, on May 22, 1874, at the church of San Marco in Milan, it was then repeated at a packed La Scala. The opera house venue permitted wild applause and encores that would have been unseemly in church; at the end, Verdi was given a silver crown.

The Austrian poet and opera librettist Hugo von Hofmannsthal once wrote of art, "Depth must be concealed. Where? On the surface." That insight has been applied to the deceptively simple and delightfully "superficial" yet profound masterpieces of Mozart. But it may also explain the enduring achievement of Verdi's *Requiem*. It all rings true, right up to that hushed final prayer "Libera me . . . Libera me." With a subtle stroke of genius, Verdi has the orchestra end quietly on a C-major chord, as if to affirm that the prayer has not been in vain.

The music producer and author George Marek summed it up best: "The *Requiem* is one of those rare religious compositions which are loved both by the faithful and the agnostic. It is also one of those pieces of music which appeal both to the musically literate and the musical beginner. Its beauty lies deep and on the surface."

I am not surprised to find that I own more recordings of Verdi's *Requiem* than of any other piece of music. There is such room for a variety of interpretations and a cornucopia of records to prove it. All the great conductors tackle this work. Yet, after decades of listening, I find myself drawn closest to that of an Italian maestro. But it is not the obvious one, Arturo Toscanini, who recorded it several times. Rather, it is Carlo Maria Giulini's 1964 studio recording with Elisabeth Schwarzkopf's definitive rendition of the *Libera Me*. In the words of the Anglican cleric and critic Alec Robertson, "Toscanini's unforgettable interpretation was, at any rate in the '*Dies Irae*' and '*Libera Me*,' full of the visionary fervour and fire of an Old Testament prophet. Giulini's belongs to the New Testament. There are stern words in the Gospels about the Last Judgment but the keynote of this [Giulini's] less austere interpretation is compassion—the compassion of Christ."

Dame Elisabeth Schwarzkopf, who had five years earlier recorded, to my ears, the consummate *Nozze di Figaro* under Giulini's baton, commented to me just a few months before she died, "He fought great battles inside himself to make it right, to find the expression, giving his utmost."

A decade later, Verdi composed the most hauntingly plaintive *Ave Maria* in the history of music: Desdemona's bedtime prayer, charged with the foreboding of danger—indeed, doom (just moments before she is strangled by her jealous husband)—in his late opera *Otello*. It conjures up in sound the Blessed Virgin with more power and presence than any spoken prayer or painted altarpiece. Music and words are perfectly matched to evoke the beauty of simple faith, a pair of velvet gloves.

An irony here must be faced: So often Verdi is described as fiercely anticlerical and agnostic, and indeed he often presented himself this way. Yet his final work, composed when he was approaching eighty-five, was his *Quattro Pezzi Sacri* (four sacred pieces), which included, along with two a cappella hymns to the Virgin (*Ave Maria* and *Laudi alla Virgine*), his late masterpieces of choral writing, the *Stabat Mater* and *Te Deum*. Compared with the equally "operatic" version of the *Stabat Mater* by Gioachino Rossini, Verdi's is distinctive in his care to underscore with meaning every phrase of that thirteenth-century poem about the Crucifixion.

The poem itself is uneven, and Rossini had farmed out to an assistant those verses he considered weaker; the result is an operatic alternation of arias and choruses. Verdi's is one seamless garment of intense narration, bringing into focus the heroism and horrors of the Crucifixion, which begins with Jesus's Mother standing full of grief by the cross on which her son has been hung (*Stabat mater dolorosa, juxta crucem lacrimosa, dum pendebat filius*) and concludes its long sequence of images and prayers with the intercession "When my body shall die, grant that my spirit may be given the glory of Paradise. Amen." The prayer is full of drama, but equally of divine compassion and humanity. The series of four pieces ends with the thunderous and glorious *Te Deum*, which Richard Osborne rightly claims as the "*Requiem*'s true sequel, a setting which ponders the heights, and scales the depths, of human yearning."

How, then, are we to describe (if not explain) Verdi: brilliant agnostic or ultimately, if paradoxically, Christian composer? The question is as old as St. John's account of Doubting Thomas and as modern as those complex characters in the novels of Graham Greene—especially the "whiskey priests" of lost faith in his novel *The Power and the Glory* and his play *The Potting Shed*. How often those very people who believe they have lost all belief end up praying and giving witness—perhaps more persuasively through the power of doubt—to the last word of faith. Often they end up being the ones who offer others the greatest inspiration, especially if they are touched by divine genius. Like Leonardo, another famous doubter, Verdi gave precise instructions for his church burial. In his case, "one priest, a candle, a cross."

Elisabeth Schwarzkopf as the Marschallin (Covent Garden, 1959)

Chapter 16

Elisabeth Schwarzkopf

Reflections at Twilight

This morning (January 30, 2006) I landed in Paris en route to Zürich, the first leg of my pilgrimage to Schruns in Vorarlberg, Austria, to visit Dame Elisabeth Schwarzkopf. She has lived in Schruns these past three years, under a glistening tiara of snow-capped Alps, ever since moving from her house in Zumikon, outside Zürich. I had hoped to time my visit to celebrate her ninetieth birthday last month, but a family obligation prevailed. So now I finally arrive on the heels of Mozart's 250th birthday.

I am sitting in an old inn called the Hemingway beside the village church of St. Jodok, so refreshing in its sorbet hues and beckoning with its confectionery onion dome atop the bell tower. It's a blessedly short stroll through snowy streets to my hotel, the Zimba, a few houses down from Schwarzkopf's flat. It's all within a stone's throw of the train station, where I was thrilled to arrive at the end of the railway. Back home, I had boasted that getting here would take two planes and four trains. I had miscalculated: The trains numbered six—a daunting itinerary to decipher. But I made it, one train at a time. When, in the early stages of apprehension, I reached Elisabeth via cell phone, I confessed that I felt like Tannhäuser setting off on his Roman pilgrimage. She directed me to raise my sights and look up at the mountains—pitch-perfect advice. Our Rockies cannot compete; these Alps take the gold. As the train passed alongside a lake outside Zürich, the fine mist rising from frigid water cast the magnificent mountain backdrop in a gray-slate haze, a Romantic veil that mirrored a Caspar David Friedrich landscape. Oscar Wilde was right: Art doesn't imitate nature; nature imitates art.

I have never written more than a postcard in a restaurant. But Hemingway's has a long wooden table with no one else at it; I might as well be sitting at my desk back home as two neighboring tables of cheerful Austrian skiers provide a steady current of melodic conversation. I recall that my family's most Ernest author used to write in cafés and in fact came to Schruns with his wife Hadley and infant son and stayed a full six months—long enough to complete his first great novel, *The Sun Also Rises*—an idyllic interlude he later chronicled at the end of *A Moveable Feast*. I was reminded of that literary footnote as I boarded my fourth train, from Buchs to Feldkirch, which would transport me from Switzerland through Liechtenstein and finally across the border into Austria. Its side was emblazoned *The Ernest Hemingway*; I knew at last I was on the right track. Hemingway's centennial had underscored the fruits of his favorite maxim: *D'abord il faut durer*—he has endured.

But today that footnote belongs to the impeccable Dame Elisabeth: At ninety she has justly been hailed the greatest singer of Mozart for the second half of the past century, certainly for my lifetime and arguably her own as well. That is my thesis to be inked on the pristine cream-colored pages of this leather-bound journal that my bride, Ritchie, gave me as a wedding gift. Its gold-stamped year, 1979, was as sad for Elisabeth as it was happy for me. That was the year her husband died just three days after her farewell concert, at the close of which he had proclaimed her "a bloody miracle." Through my five decades of listening, she has projected into sound the absolute ideal of beauty—what Shakespeare called "the constant image."

Sitting almost alone in the breakfast room of the Zimba, while most of the families have already taken to the slopes, I can see through the lightly draped picture windows the Alps and patches of the clearest blue skies I can recall. I am sure I have seen a sky as blue in Maine or even Florida, but here the backdrop of the Alps and the reflections of the snowcapped peaks work their morning magic—and long beyond first light. I have almost two hours until I walk over to Elisabeth's. Time to meander in daylight and daydream about an excursion up the mountains.

I still cannot believe that it has been twenty years since I last saw Elisabeth, whom I first met in 1981, the year my father published *On and Off the Record*, her memoir and collection of writings by her recently deceased husband, Walter Legge, the legendary record producer at EMI and arguably the past century's most influential impresario in classical music. I had escorted her around a maze of publishers at the Frankfurt Book Fair that fall and later, as my reward, attended her master classes over the next three years at the Mannes College of Music in my hometown, New York.

Fifteen years later, in 2000, we renewed a friendship via phone and fax, prompted by my arranging for a reissue of the book, for which I had the enviable assignment of choosing photographs from her collection, composing her captions in the first person (the ultimate reward for an accidental life in publishing), and thereby vicariously retracing her luminous career.

This morning, as she greets me at her door, two decades vanish in an *Augenblick*: Her face shines with expression, her eyes sparkle with wit and warmth, and her voice rings as clear in speech as on record. She directs me into her music room, awash in pale winter light. Though February is a day away, we are surrounded by flowers in full bloom, a collage of color photographs she took of the gardens her husband planted for her over the years, to welcome her home from world-ranging tours of concert and opera stages.

We are seated on an eighteenth-century love seat; in front of us, on a delicate table beside my recording equipment, is a tray of coffee and sweets. I cannot help thinking of *Der Rosenkavalier*, act one, sans libretto.

"Don't you want any cream?"

"No, thanks—tell me when to stop," I reply, adding a touch to her cup.

"More cream, please—it is not yet forbidden."

Dominating the room is a grand piano, closed but with a vocal score on top; at the side, by the glass doors, a brass music stand displays a framed photograph of Legge; another, still larger portrait of her late husband hangs on the far wall, directly facing—appraising?—the would-be pianist. I confess to Elisabeth my early obsession with Mozart; as a boy pianist, I could readily identify with Schroeder in *Peanuts*, except that the bust on my piano was of Wolfgang, not Ludwig. I used to commute back and forth from piano bench to phonograph, to listen and then try to imitate Walter Gieseking playing the simplest minuets on a classic recording of all Mozart's piano music on Angel Records, produced by—who else?—her husband.

"At least they *seemed* simple," she interjects. "Ah, Gieseking! Do you know that Gieseking, when he accompanied me on the recording of Mozart *Lieder*, never used the pedal once? That was really something unheard of—and it was perfect." The mention of the first pianist I ever heard strikes a welcome chord. "We do have to learn not to sing like the piano," she continues, "which is not a legato instrument—and it is very difficult because it is the instrument that most singers hear accompanying them. Pianists use the pedal to make it seem legato, but Gieseking didn't: He didn't touch the pedal at all; he just played and it sounded legato."

I am still thinking of Wolfgang the child prodigy and his family life in Salzburg. I ask what she thinks about the possibility of a musical gene running through families. "Not gene," she insists. "I'd rather use the word *instinct*." I ask about her parents: Which of them passed on that instinct to her? "My father took his guitar with him when he went off to fight in the First World War. He was very musical and he made me learn the guitar immediately."

Then, all of a sudden, we are back to the present: "Why did you travel so far to see me? I can't give you a performance."

"You give me a performance every day through your recordings."

"I haven't listened to a single record in this room for three years. I started one, but the acoustics were so wrong that I finished it in two minutes and never heard another."

I am aware of how important visualization has been in Schwarzkopf's artistry—she often called herself an *Augenmensch* (visual person)—which has long fascinated me as an art historian. When coaching Bach's *St. Matthew Passion*, for instance, she would have a student picture the famous crucifixion by Grünewald. She delighted especially in the landscapes of Monet—those "visible blessings of the past," as she once described them to me. But visualization was not only an internal process in crafting hues of color and light. The scene has to fit the notes.

"Is Mozart ideal training for young singers?" I wonder. "Can young singers perhaps harm themselves by singing too much Mozart too soon?"

Here she is far more reassuring. "No, Mozart is the ideal schooling for singers but in the *style* of Mozart, not of Verdi or Wagner. The fixed style of Mozartean singing has rules, things you must do and things you must on no account do."

It comes as no surprise to a Schwarzkopf fan that her touchstone is legato, that quality of seamless singing in which she is peerless.

> *You don't learn it through the piano, but through stringed instruments. . . . I played the viola—not very well, but at least I had to play it. The ear is your most important instrument in making music; the ear will tell you, "Well, that wasn't legato, that note was finished too soon, why don't I bind it, why can't*

> *I sing it in one strength out, why don't I sing as it is written in a diminuendo and then go pianissimo to the next note, legato, or sing it with a crescendo and go to a legato even in a subito piano after a crescendo?" All those things have to be learned via the ear, your own ear.*
>
> *Likewise, the singer has to put the right person into the sound—not your person, but the person that Mozart wanted to hear. It shouldn't just sound like Miss Schwarzkopf! The Cherubino voice is different from the Susanna voice—they are all different—and you have to have so many different voices in your own voice if possible—and it is not always possible—so they may still recognize me as Schwarzkopf but they should also recognize today, "Aha, that is Susanna!" or the next day, "Aha, that is the Countess!"—the same opera, but different ways of singing.*
>
> *This is what you have to learn in the* Hochschule *or with a teacher or with your own* Fantasie, *your own imagination. Imagination is the means of translating into your singing a feeling of what art is and what a great composer is. You cannot sing one piece like the next.*

Throughout her career she deliberately limited her roles—in some, she said, "the sound was not right for me" and in singing "you must do justice to the persona in Mozart's cast." One role that fit like a glove—a velvet one at that—was the Countess in *Figaro*. Elisabeth remains, for me, the definitive *Contessa*.

"It was Furtwängler who most influenced me, with the sound, with the expression you must feel the second before the note. When you talk, you alter your expression every second, every part of a second; you should do that when you sing."

"So, then, no matter how carefully crafted a performance, there is always the element of the almost instantaneous?"

"Certainly."

The recording I have listened to more times than I can count, ever since I studied it for a term as a college student, is the Giulini *Figaro*, recorded after she had been singing the Countess for a decade. It was that conductor's first recording of a Mozart opera for Legge at EMI. "Walter believed in him very much; I liked him very much. . . . We all know he fought great battles inside himself to make it right, you see, to find the expression; you could feel it—that he was giving his utmost to do the right thing and never felt safe that it was the right sound; he battled for it all the time, and that brings forth great expression from a human being." Hence the visceral excitement of a recording that has never staled in its infinite variety over decades of listening.

Speaking of battles, what about *Don Giovanni*? I read recently that whenever Schwarzkopf sang that other signature role, the opera might as well have been retitled *Donna Elvira*! "Elvira is the most dramatic role you can do—though Donna Anna needs a bigger voice," she replied. Did she ever sing Donna Anna? "The arias, yes, but not the role—no, I was really formed for Donna Elvira, I believe, because I did find—I did feel—the right expression."

Schwarzkopf's Elvira was so magnetic, so attractive—how could the Don ever have ditched her? She once tried to fight nature and make herself repulsive. "I put on a false nose and face and made her a very cruel-looking person but it didn't work at all. Besides, if you cannot make the vocal character clear to the audience without showing her, there would be no phonograph records."

My favorite photograph from the archives is a masterpiece of chiaroscuro—her blond Elvira opposite Leontyne Price's Donna Anna at Salzburg; my confession evokes a smile of happy memory. "Ah, her voice was unusually beautiful, she had great expression—it's a totally different voice from mine, totally different character—and very, very good singing; there was not a flaw, never any kind of thinking back to singing Verdi or Puccini; she sang pure

Mozart. She had the brains and the taste of a great artist. It was stylistically perfect."

To what should this be credited, I wonder? "Talent, number one. Instinct, number two. Then training is utmost." What of cultural background? "Irrelevant. I have a young Japanese singer here who sings with utmost stylistic perfection already." So does she actually think that our European heritage will move eastward? "Absolutely. They learn so fast—the Japanese, Chinese, and Korean singers—the minute you tell them something, they do it. It is quite incredible. I have never experienced anything like it. And the tradition will pass from Europe to these other countries." I can't repress a certain wistfulness, Eurocentric that I am. Schwarzkopf, however, has no such qualms.

"Not at all—because the tradition will live!"

"Is it because there they are more respectful of our tradition?"

"Not only more respectful, but talented! They have the will—and the understanding—to produce the right sound, and not just the sound but the feeling."

I reminisce about my first trip to the Frankfurt Book Fair and Wiesbaden, where I attended a performance of *Così* in a truly cozy house, an ideal intimate staging. "I did *Don Giovanni* there," Elisabeth recalls with special warmth. She had helped settle her parents in that delightful eighteenth-century spa town for their twilight years.

"Is Mozart, then, better suited to smaller houses?"

"Yes, of course, because the discussion—the recitative—in Mozart is very fast, and passes by so quickly, and is so important for details of expression; it gets lost in a huge space."

How, then, did Schwarzkopf come to learn a Viennese style of singing Mozart?

"Well, I had two years of singing in Vienna's Theater an der Wien. Many of the roles I had to learn overnight, so I really learned the Vienna style of singing in those two years. But I also had a year out in the sanitarium in the Tatra Mountains of Slovakia, recovering from tuberculosis, and I took all my music with me and spent that year lying in the woods memorizing all the parts I wanted to sing—not singing, just memorizing."

"Not every singer," I venture, "would make such an investment from such a setback."

"I think it was pure instinct."

Her teacher, Maria Ivogün, had helped make the arrangements; across the room, her smiling picture faces us atop the bookshelf, flanked by two deep cobalt vases. I mistake the photo of Ivogün for young Elisabeth: beauty plays such tricks. "Schmitt-Walter took me to her when I was a beginner at the Berlin Opera. I was already two years at the opera house, but Maria told me I had no technique, and we started with two notes; for four months we did nothing but those two notes, and then slowly we went up bit by bit, for two years."

What about Ivogün's husband, pianist Michael Raucheisen, with whom Schwarzkopf performed her first *Lieder* recitals?

"He was the most wonderful accompanist in all the world, the greatest accompanist that ever was—*punto, finito.*"

I want to turn the clock back even further, to the earliest years of study; we had both attended all boys schools—an ocean and an era apart—she due to the fact that her father was headmaster. There she learned to play a host of instruments, from the lute and glockenspiel to the organ, and she sang Mary in Christmas pageants. Years later, progressing through Mozart roles at the Deutsches Opernhaus, she began with Blondchen in *Die Entführung* and then Konstanze. In *Die Zauberflöte*, she started in the chorus—for the famous Beecham recording overseen by her future husband, Walter Legge, in 1937—and then sang one of the three boys and finally Pamina. In *Figaro*, she passed through Barbarina to Susanna and finally the Countess, the role she owned for the rest of her career.

"Which Mozart role remains the most dramatically and vocally challenging?"

"Even the slightest folk song is challenging all the time. But I would have to say Fiordiligi, which is very long and very hard to sing well. You have to hold a true position of your voice throughout, and you really don't even have a minute to go to your dressing room!"

It is now time to pretend—in the spirit of Walter Mitty—that I am her student. "What is the most important thing for a student of Mozart?"

"The timbre of the voice, the sound of the voice—it has to be an utterly beautiful sound, and not just the notes as such. That sound will vary from the secco recitatives to the accompanied ones, to the first notes at the beginning of the aria, which is again not quite the sound of the aria itself, and so on."

"After all the preparation, at the moment of singing an aria, can a singer allow herself to enjoy the emotion, of joy, sorrow, whatever, that is being conveyed to the audience?"

"No, you must be able to put your feeling into the sound and to hear what you are doing; the ear is all important."

"What of the current vogue of spontaneity, of just being yourself?"

"No, because there is the matter of style, and the style is in the music—and if Mozart hasn't got style, I don't know who has—and that style needs observation, it needs knowledge, it needs hearing, what you are doing wrong, a feeling for the tempo, for changing of color, as permitted: You don't have a lot of freedom in Mozart, but you don't have to be afraid of giving beauty to Mozart if it is true to style—and you must always obey the conductor, because Mozart is not conducted by nitwits!"

The theologian Karl Barth once quipped that in heaven Bach was court composer, but every afternoon the angels sneaked off to play Mozart. I want to know Elisabeth's appraisal of that court composer since I have long been addicted to her early recordings of his cantatas, spun with a young voice of pure silver. "Bach," she replies, "is fiendishly difficult to sing—I'd rather five times Mozart than one-half time Bach!"

Then I ask the question to which I am convinced I already have the answer: What composer, if she were allowed only one, would she keep for herself?

"Smetana."

I should know better than to second-guess Schwarzkopf. Why Smetana? "His richly loving folk sound," she replies. Her father had loved Smetana, and so does she. Even with no roots in Czech soil, she finds listening to that composer "always a kind of homecoming."

I am determined to salvage Mozart. "Surely he was the most gifted, the most ingenious of composers?"

"I don't know. I think he is the most feared to do justice to, because not doing so is immediately audible, immediately exposed."

"Why? Isn't Bach technically as difficult?"

"More difficult, but Bach does not touch you in the same way as Mozart does. Mozart is so simple, touching you immediately with just a few notes. Bach needs many more notes to touch you."

After Dame Elisabeth enumerates the grueling details of traveling, packing, unpacking, and everything that precedes performing on tour, I ask her to pretend that I am now her agent and asking her preference: a staged opera, opera in concert, or a recording?

She recalls so fondly those concert performances of Mozart operas arranged by her husband in London's Festival Hall. "You don't act across the stage, but you do react to each other. I think those are the ideal performances because you don't have to concentrate on whether that chair will break down, or whether I have the right dress, but can concentrate on singing. Those were the very best opera concerts I ever did."

"I am surprised to hear this from someone as gifted in acting as in singing."

"But, you know, you can still act while standing still. You can look and listen and react to what your partners are singing. More is not needed. In the recording studio, on the other hand, one does not have the freedom even to turn and look to the side but must stand completely still and focus on the score."

At two o'clock—or is it closer to three?—it is clearly time for a break, and Elisabeth encourages me to go to the top of the *Hochjoch* for a late lunch and for a loftier view from the mountains she has loved all her life. So I take the cable car to the top of the *Hochjoch*. Everyone else has skis; I have my camera. I have been deathly afraid of heights all my life, but today there is no turning back. I hope the film develops; the views are breathtaking.

When I take the cable car back down, I suddenly see that I am returning to late-afternoon shadow after the snow-reflecting sunlight of just minutes earlier. I've never realized how much illumination mountains steal from the valleys between them. No wonder Moses (and prophets to follow) sought and found God on a mountaintop. *Lux Umbra Dei*—light is the shadow of God.

Yet more revelations remain below. Elisabeth's eyes have been bothering her today, and when I arrive at six in the evening, she suggests that I postpone our conversation until tomorrow. But I am determined not to leave as soon as I've arrived, and so I pointedly leave the recorders in the bag and offer to do something practical for her, explaining that I have been well trained by both my mother and my wife.

She has me open a bottle of red wine for her—a "glass and a half"—and as I sip water, we talk over a range of subjects starting with religion, prompted by her framed photo of our mutual friend Cardinal Christoph Schönborn of Vienna. Elisabeth says she is a great admirer of Schönborn, whom I suggest may someday be pope. She beams as she declares, "He is very courageous; he says what he thinks." (Obviously a kindred soul.) To her protests that she considers herself "neither Protestant nor Catholic" and "hardly pious," I counter that St. Augustine said that "whoever sings prays twice." Her singing has surely given more glory to the Creator than a lifetime of kneeling in church.

We talk of Richard Strauss's librettist Hugo von Hofmannsthal, whom she considers a great poet. Elisabeth then turns to the framed photograph of her beloved father, "Poppi," and tells me of his lifelong love of books and how his treasured library had been saved in Berlin and shipped to storage in Bavaria toward the end of the war by devoted soldiers who had served under him on the Russian front, where the middle-aged classics teacher had been conscripted to identify the fallen, notify their families back home, and make the arrangements for burial.

By the end of our two-hour talk on and off the record, I ask whether I might go into the music room and play her piano alone—to see whether I might have the nerve to play for her tomorrow. She says yes but adds she will not promise not to follow me!

And so she does. Sitting opposite, she stops me measure by measure and offers the most insightful critique and piano lesson I have ever experienced. I should have practiced days, if not weeks, before coming here. What was I thinking? I sit and wait for the obvious conclusion: "No wonder you are a writer." Instead, she looks at me with clear blue eyes of wonder and asks, "Why are you not performing?"

To all my excuses—that it was a childhood pursuit, that I don't have enough talent, that it is too late, that I don't practice—she counters, "But you must play. Why do you want to write about music when you can make it? You have time to perform—do it!"

I hedge. "I would love to have been able to sing."

"But that is not your instrument. The piano is. Make *it* sing—and thank God it exists."

Before I flew over here, I wrote to my son that I felt that I was going to Schruns "to meet my fate." I was jesting in earnest. But now it is no joke: Life will never be the same. I shall go back to practice, back to musical scores, back to the keyboard of my childhood. Down deep I have always suspected that my musical laziness has taken a toll in true satisfaction, if not happiness. But it took a dame of the British Empire (and a *Kammersängerin*) to put it into words—with blunt, incredulous honesty. Our interview tomorrow will be interesting, to say the least. And I have already promised to return and play again—but only after practice.

I hardly slept at all last night. Was it the cream sauce on the pasta I had for dinner, or something less easily digested? The realization that a new route has been pointed out for me, and life will never be the same again? I cannot afford to procrastinate or rationalize. Elisabeth speaks with nine decades of experience and a life offered on the altar of music. As she remarked, music is the only holy art permitted in every church of every denomination, from Catholic to the most Protestant. I no longer have the luxury of protesting that I am out of practice. As my late dad would say, "No rush, just do it immediately."

This morning's visit to Elisabeth at eleven is far more relaxed, but it is clear from the start that I will never get her to philosophize about singing or even Mozart's roles. I hear, in the mind's ear, the echo of her Marschallin gently scolding her beloved Octavian in the early morning light: "Philosophier' Er nicht, Herr Schatz!" She is no philosopher, she protests to me, but "purely practical," and her secrets are reserved only for other singers. She discounts journalists and critics; hence her conviction that I should exchange my laptop keyboard for a holier one—the piano's.

But I explain, as I unpack the recorders, that I am no critic, nor a journalist. In fact, this is my very first interview. She is startled.

"Why did you come all this way, then?"

"As a pilgrim," I reply—to give thanks to the singer who illuminates my every week, if not day, via recordings. I came purely as a lover of her singing and of Mozart, a listener who still buys her vinyls on eBay to savor the original sound, not as a professional journalist or critic. "This interview," I explain, "was an afterthought with *Opera News*."

"Be sure to tell your readers," she instructs, and so I do.

We move into the music room, and I switch on the recorders for another two hours of discussion. I want to learn more about what she terms the "Mozart sound." Even though he wrote Italian operas, it is not an Italian sound, she explains. The Mozart sound remains constant, whether in German or Italian. So how does a young singer find it?

"They have to be taught. You know, sometimes I make students sing a sound thirty times and suddenly on the thirty-first time: 'Ah, that is the sound you are supposed to make.'"

How did she herself find it? Through her teacher Maria Ivogün, and Raucheisen, and later her husband, Walter Legge. "He had a phenomenal ear and a phenomenal idea of music, not only of Mozart but of all music."

Would she envision the sound in terms of other instruments?

"Not at all—it is enough to have to know your own instrument!"

Yet she would study the full orchestral scores when preparing a role. Violins are key, for they alone can "imitate the vibrato of the human voice." For instance, when singing a passage in which the first violins take the second voice, in accompaniment as though a duet, "you listen to that violin and try to make your voice as similar as you can to that vibrato." To me, Schwarzkopf makes opera singing sound like a chamber music ensemble.

"But of course it is—do you think it could be otherwise? You need to listen closely to the orchestra, to the solo instruments, because the mood of the aria is already set in the introduction, which offers the most revealing notes about the aria, because the aria is but the feeling of what you have said about the situation in the recitative."

"So studying the recitative is no minor matter?"

"Oh, no—it is more important than the aria!"

It is time to approach, gingerly, the heart of the matter: "Why is Mozart the most widely beloved composer? Why not Haydn or Handel, who wrote so many more operas to choose from?"

In three words, "his melodic instinct: Non-musicians can leave whistling his melodies."

Schwarzkopf is unusual among singers for her fidelity and devotion to the written texts of the librettists as the inspiration and illumination of the composer's notes. Last night, speaking of Hofmannsthal, she told me, "Everything you need to know about living life is in *Der Rosenkavalier*." So much for the singer who earlier protested that she had nothing philosophical to say, only the most practical things about the craft of singing! She remains ever my Marschallin.

What opera of Mozart's comes closest to that appraisal of Hofmannsthal?

"*Figaro*, of course."

We take a break as Elisabeth rises from the love seat to take a turn around the room. I offer to try to get her turntable turning again and play for her the record of *Messiah* highlights, produced by her husband in 1964, his last year at EMI, which I bought on eBay and brought over to add to her collection.

Her hi-fi is more complicated than any system I have ever confronted, and the large framed photo of Walter Legge does not increase my confidence. But I forge ahead and suggest we listen to "Porgi amor" from the Giulini *Figaro*, my Mozartean grail. "Would it be interesting," I ask next, "to hear the same aria recorded ten years earlier?"

"Yes, cruel but interesting."

I protest that it's surely never cruel to get younger.

"Well, I hope it is better."

I put on the 1950 Vienna recording. She was at this point moving from years of singing Susanna to the Countess; does she still hear the voice of Susanna?

"Yes, all of it . . . marvelous piano . . . it's very clean, but it's a child's voice . . . very sweet . . . but it's not ripe enough for the Countess, much too young."

When I protest that both the Countess and she were indeed young (she was then only thirty-four, the Countess perhaps a few years younger), she quips, "Well, I wasn't eighteen, you know." The Countess is wiser and should sound "riper," she concludes.

After several more selections, I have worn out my welcome with the machinery. "I think you'd better put that energy into piano playing," she laughs.

So I retreat to the piano for a second impromptu coaching session before leaving for the airport. I start with a Bach prelude in C-sharp; the piano itself is sharp, her criticism even sharper—and to the point.

"Could you make it sound like a discussion between the hands? Softer there . . . discussing . . . two people discussing, all the time . . . come in with the left hand . . . give me those four bars piano . . . ta-ta, quick . . . two people fighting, discussing." Then on to Beethoven's *Ecossaises*.

"Take an audible breath . . . can you make that an echo . . . make that less beautiful . . . more!"

I remind her that I took six trains to reach her; I will not turn back now. Her final prescription is to add more *Fantasie* to the pieces once the technique is secure. The Haydn sonata, for instance, needs "more visible humor, wit"; the repeats: more color, more variety. The Scarlatti sonata should be turned into a conversation among as many as four people.

Finally, Chopin's "L'adieu" Waltz. "Can that seem more like a viola coming in there? Start again. . . . Ah! Left hand. . . . You need more freedom. . . . You are not thinking of singing, and you should

. . . even breathing, in and out." It's not just about the notes, she stresses. "There are so many possibilities in the music: It's about adding the feelings and human reactions."

I ask whether her performances, even after years of preparation, might suddenly change.

"Absolutely, always, in a moment." She suggests I study some comic actors for the range of human reactions to be translated through the keyboard. Opera without words—or *Lieder ohne Worte*. "You should be able to work the piano music into a human expression." It is, in the end, all a matter of *Fantasie*, her favorite word, of our imagination; not only a matter of technical precision—that is just the skeleton (which of course must be sound) on which the flesh-and-blood interpretation makes a piece of music a living thing. "Music without thoughts, without ideas," she insists, "is a waste of time."

Little did I know what I would take away from this visit, which was initially intended not as an interview but a thank-you for all those years of grace and vocal paradise via recordings. We open a copy of the new edition of her Scribner book *On and Off the Record*. My favorite photo is the one of her looking upward, like a Guido Reni saint in ecstasy—not singing but "listening" (as she inscribed on the verso: "Hören!"). And that, I conclude, is the key to her success and to her vocal embodiment of the glory of Mozart, *da capo al fine*.

As we say *auf Wiedersehen*—not good-bye—and I promise to practice her lessons before returning in summertime with my wife, she tells me to waste no time getting to the keyboard. But which keyboard? Her final question, an encore from last night, gives the answer: "Why do you want to write about music when you can make it?"

I am going home by another route. I explain to Elisabeth that I would gladly take six trains to see her, but not to leave her. As I cross the music room to come around the other side of the love seat, she turns to me and says, "You know, in this light you seem about seventeen years old!" Then after a pause, she adds, "Perhaps part of you still is?" *Ja, ja*. I have always loved being a student; it is too late to give it up.

Die Zeit, die ist ein sonderbar Ding . . . Auch sie ist ein Geschöpf des Vaters der uns alle erschaffen hat. Time is a strange thing . . . yet it, too, is a creation of the Father who made us all. So sings my favorite Marschallin on record.

Frederica von Stade as Octavian (San Francisco Opera, 1993)

Chapter 17

Frederica von Stade

Flicka in the Firmament

Flicka's debut at the Met—as one of the three Genies (or *Sängerknaben*) in Mozart's *Die Zauberflöte*—was a big deal for her Far Hills fans from New Jersey. She was our shooting star. Her grandmother and namesake, Frederica Clucas (known as Freddy), was a longtime friend of my grandmother Vera Scribner; her mother, Sara, was a close childhood friend of my late aunt Julia; her late father, Charlie von Stade, had been at St. Paul's with my dad, who said that he had by far the best singing voice in the school. I was a Princeton freshman that winter of 1970 and often commuted back and forth to New York to take advantage of the weekday evening opera subscription my parents had bought for my benefit. I recall being taken backstage afterward by a group of grande dames and gents to see Flicka in her dressing room. Forget Pamina, Papagena, and the Queen: Flicka was the Star of the Night.

That experience was duplicated the following October when she sang Flora alongside Joan Sutherland's Violetta in *La Traviata*. Verdi may have written his best and brightest notes for Violetta, with Flora in a modest supporting role, but whenever those two ladies shared the stage, all eyes were on Flora. Even when she was silent, Flicka commanded the stage with her sheer presence and dramatic authenticity; she didn't need notes to soar above the crowd.

I first heard Flicka sing Cherubino in *Figaro* the winter of 1975 at the Met, a couple of years after she captured in Paris that role for a lifetime. I was soon able to enjoy it afresh on a record, a vinyl I still treasure and replay on one of my many turntables. (Yes, I also have a rotary phone.) It was her first released album, a joint song recital with soprano Judith Blegen. Flicka's signature "Non so più" (from *Figaro*) on that album was the first time Mozart's newly discovered manuscript of that sprightly aria at the Morgan Library in New York had ever been recorded: Mozart himself had rearranged it for an intimate chamber performance by soprano, violin, and piano. *Non novum sed nove*—not something new, but heard in a new way. Was it ever.

By the end of the year, I was back at the Met for a December matinee, hearing—and seeing—the magical combination of Flicka's Cherubino alongside Kiri Te Kanawa, the most impeccable Countess since Elisabeth Schwarzkopf. The trouser role seemed to have been written for Flicka. Perhaps it was: What difference in God's eyes does a couple of centuries make? It's one of those instances—profoundly subjective and yet objectively defensible—when a performer takes ownership of a role for a lifetime. For me, Flicka owns Cherubino, just as Elisabeth Schwarzkopf personifies Strauss's Marschallin, or Mary Costa, Puccini's Musetta.

One of my favorite recordings is Flicka's 1977 *Rosenkavalier* with Evelyn Lear as her Marschallin and Ruth Welting as Sophie. Flicka remains my favorite Octavian of all time. Indeed, my lasting operatic regret is that I never saw her perform ("sing" sounds too limited) the part. My ultimate wish, in a parallel universe, would be to pair her with my definitive Marschallin, Elisabeth Schwarzkopf, who retired from her signature role years before Flicka sang the dashing young Count. To be sure, to have a Marschallin thirty years older than her lover would be stretching more than vocal cords.

Soon afterward, it was a surprise blessing to have Flicka as a neighbor on Long Island in the 1980s. There, quite by chance, I met her coach and accompanist Mason Senft one day at her house. He soon became my piano coach—and later vocal coach for the year I volunteered as a weekday cantor at St. Patrick's Cathedral.

Albert Einstein said, "Coincidence is God's way of remaining anonymous." My father's last breath coincided with the conclusion of Flicka's recording of *Show Boat* playing at his bedside—his favorite musical. Seventeen years later, my mother breathed her last to the heavenly sound of Flicka's Maria von Trapp (on Mom's favorite CD, *The Sound of Music*), singing, "So long, farewell, *auf Wiedersehen*, good-bye."

The last time I heard Flicka sing at the Met was a dozen years earlier, in 2000, when she starred in its premiere of Lehár's *The Merry Widow*, with Domingo as her Danilo. The last time I saw her in person was a decade later when she came to New York to be the honoree at the Metropolitan Opera Guild's 2010 annual luncheon at the Waldorf Astoria. I was co-chairman of that memorable celebration and got a ringside seat together with our most musical Cardinal Edward Egan leading the cheers for the brightest and warmest star in the firmament. As Fitzgerald wrote, "If it wasn't life, it was magnificent."

Having spent most of my life in book publishing, by an accident of birth, I have read many biographies of musical stars from the stages of opera to concert halls. I have long yearned for a biography of Flicka, a doubly daunting challenge in both words and images, with such a subject whose beauty matches her talent.

Finally it has been met, surpassing all hopes, by Richard Parlour's spectacular book *Flicka* (2026), which chronicles her life and career with dazzling photographs. I cannot think of another musical biography that combines such impeccable research with engaging prose and captivating imagery. It is more than a beautiful book; it is a treasure. To have played even a C-minor part in its production—mainly accompanying the author with timely cheers—has been, for me, the icing on the cake of a life in books.

Mary Costa in her 1964 Met Opera debut as Violetta

Chapter 18

Mary Costa

A Star That Sparkles

In the fall of 1977, I got an unusual invitation from the Metropolitan Opera's assistant manager Francis Robinson (nicknamed "Mr. Met") to be his guest at "Pipe Night" at the Players Club in New York. He had arranged the evening's entertainment by three opera stars; two of them, the tenor and baritone, sat at the table with us. The third, soprano Mary Costa, was singing Musetta at the Met that month; she was Francis's longtime friend and fellow Tennessean.

By divine coincidence, I had heard her sparkling voice on the radio several days earlier—my first night at my own apartment. I was listening to my favorite classical music station, WQXR, which was broadcasting live from Carnegie Hall. Francis was the announcer on stage and gave an introduction so arresting that I have stolen it for toasts ever since: "Someone once asked Noel Coward, 'Mr. Coward, what do you have to do to be a star?' His answer was one word, 'Sparkle.' Mary Costa sparkles; she also sings." Did she ever. First, Richard Strauss's soaring aria "Zweite Brautnacht" (Second Wedding Night) from his opera *The Egyptian Helen*, and then Franz Lehár's aria "Ich bin so Verliebt" (I'm So Loved) from his operetta *Schön ist die Welt* (How Fair the World). Was she ever.

Mary was upstairs resting in Edwin Booth's bedroom as we all listened to a rare recording (from a wax cylinder) of the famous actor—and brother of Abraham Lincoln's assassin—reciting Shakespeare. Francis was irritated that his star soprano was still upstairs, and so he sent me to fetch her. I climbed halfway up and then decided I was not about to invade her privacy. I called out and explained that Francis was concerned about her. She replied that she was just avoiding a room full of smokers and would be down shortly—through the kitchen to the stage. I returned to the table and reported that the soprano would be down on time: "They're just stringing the wire for her to make a dramatic entrance."

Mary sang Violetta's aria and duet "Libiamo" from *La Traviata*. We were all swept away. On the cab ride with Francis back to her hotel, she and I (trying to be gallant) struggled over who would hold her suitcase. I asked her whether I might be on the list to visit her backstage after one of her *La Bohème* performances; I went to them all, and backstage too. At one of them, I brought along our famous English author P. D. James, who had come over at my father's invitation to go on a national tour organized for her latest Adam Dalgliesh mystery and first best seller, *Death of an Expert Witness*. We presented Musetta with a signed copy in her dressing room after the performance. The next night at dinner, the new "Queen of Crime"—and future Baroness James—announced to my parents (I was at the opera) that there was something brewing backstage. I was clueless; Phyllis was the master of clues. She was two months ahead of me.

Mary soon became my musical muse and was responsible for my reading Marcia Davenport's first Scribner novel, *Of Lena Geyer*. She told me on my first visit to Beverly Hills that she had once been approached by a producer at Paramount to star in a film of it. She declined; the part was for a dark European diva (Maria Callas would have been perfect). Mary was an all-American blonde from Tennessee. But out of curiosity I got the Scribner Library paperback as soon as I was back in New York and read it nonstop. Then, during that bicoastal year of 1978, I read all of Marcia's other novels on the plane back and forth to Los Angeles between Mary's opera and concert tours. Marcia's mother, the great Metropolitan Opera soprano Alma Gluck, who sang with Caruso and recorded one of the first records to sell a million copies, would have approved.

Mary's meteoric musical career—on and off the opera stages—defined all-American. Born and raised in Knoxville, she moved with her parents to Los Angeles to complete her studies at the Conservatory of Music. Then she auditioned for Walt Disney to star as Princess Aurora in his upcoming animated film, the most lavish of them all, *Sleeping Beauty*. He signed her up immediately. More generations of children—and their parents—have heard that voice than any other opera diva's. She had a stunning, God-given coloratura long before her formal training.

The opera world is full of stars who aspire to "cross over" into popular music—in television, on records, on Broadway. Mary never had to cross over: She bridged the art forms from the beginning. Her career on television and in film predated her journey to the concert and opera stages. Her most sparkling performance with Bing Crosby of their "Jingle Bells" medley made television history and still rings out a half century later (on YouTube). Mary's earlier operatic "debut" was singing the aria "Un bel di" from *Madama Butterfly* on *The Jack Benny Show*. Her big break came a few years later, in the summer of 1957, when she was called to substitute for Elisabeth Schwarzkopf at the Hollywood Bowl in a Viennese concert conducted by Carmen Dragon.

The rave reviews—one titled "Mary Costa Scores in Bold Debut"—prompted, a few months later, the debut in her first staged opera, Smetana's *The Bartered Bride*, in Los Angeles. Its director, Carl Ebert, then took her several thousand miles—and an ocean—away to Britain's Glyndebourne Festival, which he had cofounded in 1934, to star in its premiere of Wolf-Ferrari's opera *The Secret of Susanna*. The secret? She smoked! That triumph, in turn, prompted Leonard Bernstein to cast her as the lead, Cunégonde, in the American tour of his opera *Candide*—followed by the London production.

Mary's home stage for years was the San Francisco Opera, where, under the baton of Kurt Herbert Adler, she starred as Titania in the North American premiere of Britten's *A Midsummer Night's Dream* and Stravinsky's *The Rake's Progress*—a role premiered a decade earlier in Venice by . . . Elisabeth Schwarzkopf! Yet her largest audience ever was for a television solo at the West Coast memorial service two days after President Kennedy's assassination.

Jackie had personally requested that Mary sing the *Libera Me* from Verdi's *Requiem*. The soprano had less than two days to learn it for that Sunday performance at the Los Angeles Memorial Sports Arena. Conducted by the young Zubin Mehta, it was broadcast worldwide via Telstar. Never—before or after—has Verdi's masterpiece been heard by so many millions. Immediately afterward she was whisked across town by a police escort to the Sunday matinee of *La Bohème*. The curtain had to be delayed for her entrance as Musetta in Act II, as my childhood keyboard hero Van Cliburn told me some thirty years later. He was in the audience.

Mary's debut at the Met came six weeks later—as Violetta in *La Traviata*, which she had just filmed in London for the BBC television production (in English), directed by Carl Ebert's son, Peter, who had earlier directed her at Glyndebourne. That Met debut was one of the most celebrated ever by an American soprano—an all-too-rare combination of vocal agility, dramatic powers, and sheer beauty. She would go on to star there as Massenet's Manon, Verdi's Alice Ford, Johann Strauss's Rosalinde, and Samuel Barber's Vanessa—before I heard her Musetta live twenty years later. One reviewer lauded her "kilowatts of energy" that lit up the stage, "sunlight made audible."

Mary's *Traviata* had been such a success with the British public that the BBC decided to follow it, four years later, with a far grander production (in color this time) of Lehár's *The Merry Widow*. Two of the greatest Shakespeareans of all time, Sir John Gielgud and Sir Laurence Olivier, had earlier been watching the filming of *Traviata* offstage. When they learned of the plans for *The Merry Widow*, they contacted their young colleague Jeremy Brett and insisted that he take voice lessons at once to star opposite her. In his recent role as Freddy Eynsford-Hill, opposite Audrey Hepburn in the 1964 musical film *My Fair Lady*, his singing had been dubbed—by Mary's former prince in *Sleeping Beauty*, Bill Shirley! Brett followed through, and the resulting telecast was not only his greatest performance prior to Sherlock Homes but also the finest film ever of that beloved operetta—pure champagne. Costa and Brett made an irresistible couple. It was rebroadcast on the following Christmas Eve in the United Kingdom—a favorite of the queen's.

Mary was no less a triumph in Russia. Her 1970 tour of the Soviet Union, at the height of the Cold War, was so successful that she was held over for an extra two weeks. No American musician since Van Cliburn had been so embraced by the Russians. She could thaw any frozen relations. Her Viennese magic was then transferred to the wide screen in technicolor for MGM's last major musical, *The Great Waltz*, in 1972, in which she starred as Johann Strauss Jr.'s sparkling wife, soprano Jetty Treffz. If the grandiose settings, filmed on location in Vienna, overshadowed the dialogue and drama, her performance soared above it all.

Back home, the next year, Mary performed at a White House state dinner, an occasion recalled so fondly, twenty years later, to me in a letter by President Richard Nixon as one of the "high points" of his White House years. After her retirement from the stage, she turned her charisma to teaching, mentoring, and inspiring a new generation of music students in her native Knoxville, where she had launched its new opera company in 1973 with her performance, once again, as Violetta in *La Traviata*.

Then, in 2002, she was nominated to the board of the National Endowment for the Arts. I was asked to write a letter of recommendation to President George W. Bush. His aide—I was later told—took my letter into the Oval Office and digested it into one sentence (as was this president's preference): "Mr. Scribner writes that Mary Costa went from being Disney's Sleeping Beauty to an opera star at the Met and stages all over the world." His reply was even briefer: "There you go!"

Two decades later, she received the National Medal of Arts. There you go.

Envoi

Home by Another Route

My field was—and remains—the Baroque: Caravaggio, Rubens, Bernini. Yet, surprisingly, the most memorable visual artist in my professional life was thoroughly modern: Louise Nevelson. In 1976, my father published her book of memoirs, *Dawns + Dusks*. The next year, her sculptural chapel for Saint Peter's Church at the Citicorp Center was unveiled to rave reviews. I loved it. To this day I consider it the finest modernist chapel on this side of the Atlantic, a worthy successor to Matisse's Rosaire Chapel in Vence.

Nevelson's serene white wooden relief sculptures combine her characteristic abstraction with evocative Christian iconography—by a Jewish artist, for a Lutheran church—intended to appeal to visitors of all faiths; she herself called it a spiritual "oasis." I wanted our 1978 Scribner Library paperback to feature a stunning black-and-white photograph of Louise standing within her chapel; it remains to this day one of my favorite book covers. At lunch after the photo shoot, I asked Louise, cluelessly, "Are your eyelashes artificial?" (Her signature flourish, they measured more than an inch.) "*Everything* about me is artificial," she replied. Now her turn, she asked, "Tell me, Charles, is this the real world we are in?" An impossible question. I would sound either lacking in spiritual imagination or demented. After a pause, I said, tentatively,

"Well, I'm not sure, Mrs. Nevelson, but I think it's the closest we'll come to it in this lifetime." She smiled with approval.

In hindsight, that chapel (a fusion of Jewish, Early Christian, Lutheran, and secular spirituality) had more influence on my own spiritual journey than I was aware of—until now. I would surely not have focused on those Baroque giants of Catholic art had I not myself become a Roman as a college undergraduate. That move provided both a foundation and perspective on sacred art during that tumultuous century of Reformation and Counter-Reformation. Yet, when my "spiritual journal" *The Shadow of God* was published twenty years ago, I experienced a cancellation that prompted years of reappraisal.

The Roman Catholic television network EWTN, the largest worldwide, had booked an interview with me. Then they canceled it, with no explanation. When, out of curiosity, I asked my editor, Michelle Rapkin, to inquire why, she told me that the network's board had read my book and decided it was "not Catholic enough." I quipped back, "I'll take that as a compliment." To be fair, I had indeed written with admiration and gratitude about my Episcopalian upbringing, along with several non-Catholic theologians—Reinhold Niebuhr, Paul Tillich, C. S. Lewis, and Martin Buber. My favorite Catholic writers, Graham Greene and Andrew Greeley, were both considered suspicious by ultraconservatives in Rome and at home. Guilty as charged, I reluctantly conceded.

I now conclude that the EWTN board did me a huge favor. They prompted me to take an inventory of beliefs and preferences. Today I feel a renewed appreciation and affection for the Episcopal Church of my youth—the church of my wife, older son, and grandchildren. I consider it "Edited Catholicism." (And I believe in editing.) I still cherish the glories that Catholicism contributed to art, music, and literature—as these essays reflect. Yet, in the light of approaching dusk, denominational differences blend into an essential unity: "One Lord, one Faith," as St. Paul proclaimed to the Ephesians.

At the 1965 memorial service for Martin Buber, held in the landmarked Central Synagogue across Lexington Avenue from Nevelson's chapel, our most famous theological author, Paul Tillich, said in his eulogy, "We all approach the same God, but on separate paths." Home by another route.

Notes for Further Reading

(Sources, with footnotes, are available on my website at www.charlesscribner.com.)

Preface

See "Coda" in my spiritual journal *The Shadow of God: A Journey Through Memory, Art, and Faith* (New York: Doubleday, 2006); the Bernini window is discussed in my monograph *Bernini* (New York: Abrams, 1991) (for the revised paperback reprint in 2014, see my website).

Chapter 1

This essay first appeared as the introduction to Charles Scribner Jr., *In the Web of Ideas: The Education of a Publisher* (New York: Scribners, 1993). For more about my father, see his memoir *In the Company of Writers: A Life in Publishing* (New York: Scribners, 1991).

Chapter 2

Published in *Opera News* (December 1999) for the premiere of John Harbison's opera *The Great Gatsby* at the Metropolitan Opera. See also chapters 1 and 6 of my book *Scribners: Five Generations in Publishing* (Essex, CT: Lyons Press, 2023).

Chapter 3

Published in 1982 as the introduction to the Scribners editions of Fitzgerald's novel *Tender Is the Night.*

Chapter 4
Published as an introduction to the Easton Press twenty-fifth-anniversary deluxe edition of Scribners' 1969 biography *Hemingway: A Life Story* by Carlos Baker; reprinted in 1999 by the Princeton University Library in its exhibition catalog for Hemingway's centennial. See also C. Scribner Jr.'s *In the Web of Ideas* and his publishing memoir *In the Company of Writers.*

Chapter 5
Published in the October 1983 issue of *Vanity Fair* (illustrated), 60–61; see also my book *Scribners* for more on Wolfe and his publisher.

Chapter 6
Published in the *Wall Street Journal*, Saturday/Sunday, December 21/22, 2024. For more on Marcia Davenport's novels, see *Scribners.*

Chapter 7
For the illustrated version, as well as a YouTube video of my 2008 Metropolitan Museum lecture, see "Caravaggio" on my website. My illustrated and footnoted 1977 *Art Bulletin* article on Caravaggio's *Supper at Emmaus*—reprinted in the 1983 anthology *Art, Creativity, and the Sacred*—is also available on that website; also discussed in my monograph *Sacred Muse: A Preface to Christian Art and Music* (Lanham, MD: Rowman & Littlefield, 2023).

Chapter 8
My 1991 talk at the Clarence Dillon Library in Bedminster, New Jersey, is on my website, along with my two monographs *Rubens* (1989) and *Bernini* (1991). They can be read for free (on Scribd) via links on the website, which also has a link to my original article, "Rubens and Bernini," published in the *Journal of the John and Mable Ringling Museum of Art* in 1983—a comparative study, illustrated and with footnotes, of the two Baroque giants. For my recent

reconstruction of Rubens's *Eucharist* tapestries, see "The Solution" afterword to the revised 2014 paperback edition of my 1983 monograph *The Triumph of the Eucharist*—via a link on my website.

Chapter 9

The illustrated article published in the 2013 *IFAR Journal* 14, nos. 1–2, is found on my website along with YouTube links to the television documentaries *The Rubens Robbers* (BBC, 2003) and *Miami Sting* (Sky TV, 2007), as well as the taping of my 2009 Metropolitan Museum lecture.

Chapter 10

First published and lavishly illustrated as "Michelangelo's Encore" in *Arts & Antiques* (December 1991), 50–60, 99. See also *Sacred Muse*.

Chapter 11

Published online with illustrations and footnotes as "Velázquez and St. Teresa: The Lord Among Pots and Pans," *Church Life Journal* (University of Notre Dame), September 22, 2021 (link on my website).

Chapter 12

Published with illustrations and footnotes in *Proceedings of the American Philosophical Society* 135, no. 4 (1991), 490–509 (link on my website). For the rediscovered *Bust of the Savior*, see my 2014 revised paperback edition of *Bernini* (link on my website), as well as my later article "*Imago Christi*: Bernini *Saviours*, Lost and Found," *Valori Tattili* 9 (2017), 49–59 (text and link to illustrated article with footnotes on my website).

Chapter 13

For footnotes and illustrations, see "Bernini's *Cristo Vivo*," *Princeton University Art Museum Record* 77–78, nos. 2017–18 (2021), 15–23 (link on my website).

Chapter 14

For the original article, with footnotes and illustrations, see "The Garden of Love: Heaven-on-Earth in Baroque Art," in *The Incarnate Imagination: Essays in Theology, the Arts and Social Sciences*, edited by I. H. Shafer (Bowling Green, KY: Popular Press, 1988), 124–49 (link on website).

Chapter 15

From my 2023 book *Sacred Muse*.

Chapter 16

First published as "The Voice of Mozart: Elisabeth Schwarzkopf at Ninety," *Opera News* (July 2006), 16–21. The full version was published as "Epilogue: A Pilgrimage to Schruns," in *Elisabeth Schwarzkopf: From Flower Maiden to Marschallin* by Kirsten Liese, translated and edited by Charles Scribner III (New York: Amadeus Press, 2008), 141–57 (text on website). My corrective revision of her early life in wartime Berlin, "Elisabeth Schwarzkopf: Confronting a Calumny," *The New Criterion* 42, no. 9 (May 2024), is available online and on my website.

Chapter 17

My foreword to Richard Parlour's 2026 illustrated biography *Flicka: The Life and Music of Frederica von Stade* (Amazon).

Chapter 18

See my 2023 book *Scribners*, 163–64. Both the "Libera Me" from the 1963 JFK Memorial Service and the 1968 BBC *The Merry Widow* may be viewed on YouTube.

Envoi

See *Sacred Muse* and my spiritual journal *Home by Another Route* (New York: Paulist Press, 2016).

Acknowledgments

To my good friend and editor, Michelle Rapkin, I owe once again—in this fifth book under her expert care—enormous thanks for her impeccable judgment matched by perfect pitch for prose and an eagle eye for errors. She remains the ideal editor's editor—from dawn to dusk. At Lyons Press, I am again indebted to an all-star publishing team: editorial director (and fellow Princetonian) Eugene Brissie; assistant managing editor Patricia Stevenson; copyeditor Jennifer Kelland; cover designer Piper Wallis; compositor Rhonda Baker; and Shana Capozza in marketing. They uphold the best of the publishing tradition. Finally, and above all, to my wife, Ritchie, I owe far more than a dedication: But for her transplanting this hothouse New Yorker to a Florida barrier island each winter, this book (along with the two preceding ones) would not have been written.